This project takes the personal and intimate craft of memoir and turns it over to the cut-and-paste transformation of remix culture combined with a hint of old-fashioned parlour games.

Five writers have written a short piece of memoir, a vignette. Each work is passed onto another author within the group, tasked with transforming the piece into something else. In the background, if:book tracks the changes. The newly minted remix is passed along again and so on until each of the pieces have passed through all five authors.

It's called *Lost in Track Changes*.

Lost in Track Changes

CATE KENNEDY
RYAN O'NEILL
FIONA CAPP
ROBERT HOGE
KRISSY KNEEN

if:

First published by if:book Australia 2014
PO Box 3488, South Brisbane, Queensland
Second edition published by Simon Groth 2019

Cover design by George Saad
Icon artwork by Benjamin Portas

Creator: Capp, Fiona, author
Title: Lost in track changes / Fiona Capp, Robert Hoge, Cate Kennedy, Krissy Kneen, Ryan O'Neill (original texts and remixes); Simon Groth (introduction)
ISBN: 978-0-6483746-1-9
Subjects: Biographical fiction
Plot-your-own stories.
Other Creators/Contributors: Hoge, Robert, author; Kennedy, Cate, author; Kneen, Krissy, 1968- author; O'Neill, Ryan, author; Groth, Simon, editor, writer of introduction.
Dewey Number: A823.082

Subscribe to *marginalia*: an email newsletter
about reading and writing in a connected world.
simongroth.com/newsletter

Contents

Introduction

Cross this sentence out. Go on. Actually, while you're at it, cross this whole paragraph out. This is a ridiculous way to introduce a book. I'm sure you can do a better job. See all this white space around? That's your space. It's there just for you. Take up a pen (or a pencil if you're chicken) and make some notes in the margins. Write whole new sentences. Or maybe you'd prefer to subtly change the ones that are already here. That's what this book is for. Make it your own. Add your name to the cover if you like. See, this is not really a book of literary remixes, but a starting point for your own creative work. At least it could be. So, what do you think? Are you game?

I know, I know. I'm getting ahead of myself. I have a job to do. I am supposed to introduce *Lost in Track Changes*. I am supposed to give you some broad idea of what the project is about and why it's important. And I will. But the idea of a beige, official-sounding introduction really doesn't fit with the rest of this book. The five authors that follow my warm up act here produced some stunning literary acrobatics for you. Just wait. It's going to be awesome. As ringmaster[1], my role is to provide the framing necessary to give you a sense of how this works, but also to set the tone. With the fourth wall now a pile of rubble and our 'meta' credentials in place, I think we can consider it set. Okay? Okay.

Some time in 2013, Krissy Kneen proposed an idea for a project to me: ask a small group of authors to write a short work of memoir, then have them pass the work around to each other for remixing in series until each story had been modified by all. Think of it like the old game of Chinese Whispers only with digital files and literary remixes. It was an intriguing idea, not least because tying the project to memoir brought a personal and emotional punch to what would have otherwise been a purely intellectual exercise. We would be asking the authors to offer up a small piece of themselves to be chopped up, warped, and scattered by the others.

The prospect of five authors remixing each other's work in word processors suggested the additional element of tracking the changes between each version and, as part of if:book's program for 2014, *Lost in Track Changes* took its current form.

---

[1] I've never considered myself 'ringmaster' before. Maybe I should get a top hat.

I keep referring to the term 'remix', which we have of course borrowed[2] from popular music. Now I'm assuming you're comfortable with what it means in the music world, but in literature, maybe you're a little fuzzy[3]. One thing worth noting is that remixing is distinct from editing. An edit seeks to strengthen and clarify the original author's intention. A remix is made with the understanding that the remixer will intentionally change the original work as a creative act. Though a good remix contains recognisable traces of its source material, it is a wholly new work and its authorship is shared. The remix is a uniquely modern art, storytelling born of the digital age. A remix is not a 'cover version' or a reinterpretation. It's not fan fiction. In music, it couldn't exist without the advent of multitrack recording. Similarly, in literature, I would argue that remixing is the product of writing in software, of the word processor and of cut-and-paste.

Remixing is also an inherently critical act. Like it or not, the choices you make in your remixes of this book – the choices of what to keep and what to change – counter the original author's vision for the work. Some of the

---

[2] Or pinched.

[3] If you're not, you can always cross this paragraph out too.

authors struggled with the thought that they might be making value judgements of each other's writing. But any given remix need not be considered an improvement or detraction. It doesn't replace the source material. It's just different. It's a new version.

The five authors in this volume – Fiona Capp, Robert Hoge, Cate Kennedy, Krissy Kneen and Ryan O'Neill – are among the finest writers I've had the pleasure to work with[4]. We worked feverishly over a month in 2014 – a weekly turnaround – to create these stories. I say 'we': they were doing all the writing, I was keeping track of who had what and when, editing the incoming stories and dispatching the outgoing ones to the next in line. I think I had a much easier time of it, just quietly. The authors were working blind: they had no provenance for the pieces they would receive, no idea whose hands it had passed through on its way to them and no idea where it would subsequently go. This makes the evolution of each story through *Lost in Track Changes* all the more extraordinary. Sometimes changes are subtle: language becomes tighter and the text sparser. Sometimes the changes are dramatic: the whole text brushed aside or manipulated beyond recognition, perspective

---

[4] Do I say that about all my authors? Probably, but I mean it every time.

shifted or even the form itself changed completely. For some stories, the final remix retains elements of its original incarnation. Others would be unrecognisable without the steps between.

Creating a print edition of *Lost in Track Changes* was never a given. The project was first published to the web where the stories are presented with the track changes retained in all their ghastly glory for you to analyse and interrogate. The ebook edition of *Lost in Track Changes* similarly presents these changes *au naturel.* In putting together this volume, we faced some difficult questions around what purpose print serves and how it could best represent a project that took place entirely within software. We wanted to give you a sense of the changes between each remix without forcing you to wade through pages of typographical soup. After all, 'track changes' is a word processing feature that gives little thought to aesthetics; it's all function and no form. The stories are presented here with their journeys in mind: the five incarnations for each story in chronological order and, between each, a snapshot of the changes in progress.

But remember, the text that follows is only the beginning of *Lost in Track Changes.* The rest is up to you. To quote from a novel that quotes from a dirty joke[5]: 'Keep your hat on, Buster. We may wind up miles from here.'

Simon Groth

Brisbane, October 2014

[5] I was going to credit the novel, but maybe I'll leave it for you to find for yourself. It's not difficult.

In Front of Kmart by Cate Kennedy

Five days before Christmas, I was sitting on a plastic bench outside Kmart in a shopping mall, gathering strength for the onslaught of buying gifts nobody wanted or needed from department stores I usually did anything to avoid entering.

A young harassed mother near me was losing the plot with her young son.

The kid was about four and was clearly feeling as rattled, exhausted and overwhelmed as everyone else trudging around – or at least, as I was.

Christmas carol muzak swamped the air. The young Kmart staff, while remaining stony-faced, sported synthetic Santa hats as they manhandled boxes of crap across the registers.

It had been a lean year financially, one I had spent away from Australia living in a far poorer country, which I was missing so deeply I felt almost immobilised with the sense that I'd made a terrible mistake in returning. The last place in the world I wanted to be at that moment was outside a megastore glittering with tinsel and merchandise, watching a young woman grab her little boy by the arm and start shouting at him.

'Listen to me!' she yelled, her face close to his. 'That's it! We're going home now, do you hear me?'

She shifted her massive plastic bags of Christmas shopping out of her way with her leg so she could give him a good shake. The boy tried to direct his eyes somewhere else, out of the line of fire of her furious glare. Maybe she expected more resistance from him. Maybe she thought the idea of going home, far away from this wonderland of noise and toys, would make him crack and start crying and pleading. When it didn't, her fury increased. She tightened her grip on his arm and shook him again.

'Santa's not coming,' she shouted. 'Santa hates you.'

The little boy went very still. He closed down.

Nothing stopped for him, not his mother's hysterical frustration, not the grim strangers striding all around him, not 'Mary's Boy Child' inanely looping on the mall tannoy. It all just went on around him as he absorbed this blow, like a child on a street in the wake of a detonation; deafened, stunned, eyes wide, the world blown open.

I stood up and walked over to them. I put my hand on the mother's shoulder. 'You need a break,' I said. 'You don't mean that. I know you don't. Here – let me take your little boy for a while and you have a break in that café there. Just sit in there and rest and I'll take him for a walk outside and find a tree somewhere and sit under it. Then later you can say sorry and go home and wrap up these presents together and put them under the tree. How does that sound?'

No, I didn't. Of course I didn't. I caught my husband's eye and knew he shared my unhappiness at being back in Australia, caught here in the very vortex of commercialism we both despised, witnessing something so miserable that it flooded us both with fresh misery.

I haven't mentioned my husband sitting there until now, but let me paint him into the scene now. I need this for context, for narrative, to make you understand why I didn't rise to my feet, propelled by righteous anger and a larger, calmer compassion, and approach that seething young woman at the very end of her tether. I looked over at him and for a second the notion of standing up and intervening hung between us, then I felt a wave of pure despair. It held me in place like an undertow.

Believe me, I feel with you the narrative lockstep which now requires me to expand on this despair, to illustrate how this vignette is now progressing accordingly to mention that our marriage was teetering at that point, limping along on the baldest of tyres, almost out of gas. That we had no energy in ourselves to alleviate each other's misery, that we had lost the power and the will to do so. To turn this story to our endless true subject: myself. To make this boy and his mother bit-players in a drama about a faltering marriage, to show how this moment was the all-important tipping point, then moving on to the Me Show – the two of them nothing more than extras. Catalysts. It's typical of life, I am sure you will agree, to provide us with our turning-point catalysts outside Kmart, to allow us to use others in this way.

Wait. I don't want to go there. I stood up. I walked over to the mother and her son. The mother – somehow, implausibly, I'll work on this part later – allowed me to crouch down in front of her son, ignoring her, and speak to him.

'It's not you,' I said to the white-faced, trembling little boy. 'You're fantastic. Do you hear me? You're a great kid. Don't worry – your mum's under a lot of stress and adults say lots of crazy things they wish they hadn't said later. Ok? Remember what I'm telling you. It's not you.'

No, I didn't. You know I didn't. The moment hung there, the chance to change the narrative. I assessed the energy and grief and courage it would require, to thresh and flounder against that debilitating undertow and stand up and do it.

I looked over at my husband, lost in his own immobilising grief.

I'll tell you, although I don't need to now, that the relationship crashed and burned a few short months later. It's enough that you know that I'm left with this – myself sitting, doing nothing, and that boy would be eighteen now and I think of him all the time. I can tinker with the script all I like but this is the story I'm left with. Had I risen, I would have been the catalyst. I would have been someone else's turning point.

Had I risen, I wonder if I would even have had to write this now.

~~Five days before Christmas,~~ I was sitting on a plastic bench outside Kmart in a shopping mall~~, gathering strength for the onslaught of buying gifts nobody wanted or needed from department stores I usually did anything to avoid entering.~~. Five days before Christmas.

A young harassed mother near me was losing the plot with her young son.

The kid was about four ~~and was clearly feeling as~~, rattled, exhausted ~~and overwhelmed~~, as everyone else trudging around ~~– or at least, as I was.~~.

Christmas carol muzak swamped the air. The ~~young~~ Kmart staff~~, while remaining stony-faced,~~ sported synthetic Santa hats ~~as they manhandled~~, stony-faced, manhandling boxes ~~of crap~~ across the registers.

~~It had been a lean year financially, one I had spent away from Australia living in a far poorer country, which I was missing so deeply I felt almost immobilised with the sense that I'd made a terrible mistake in returning. The last place in the world I wanted to be at that moment was outside a megastore glittering with tinsel and merchandise, watching a young woman grab her little boy by the arm and start shouting at him.~~

'Listen to me!' she yelled, her face close to his. 'That's it! We're going home *now*, do you hear me?'

She shifted her massive plastic bags of Christmas shopping ~~out of her way with her leg so she could give~~, gave him a good shake. The boy tried to direct his eyes somewhere else, out of the line of fire of her furious glare. Maybe she expected more resistance from him. Maybe she thought the idea of going home, far away from this wonderland of noise and toys, would make him ~~crack and start crying and pleading. When it didn't, her fury increased.~~ cry and plead. She tightened her grip on his arm and shook him again.

'Santa's *not coming*,' she shouted. 'Santa *hates* you.'

The little boy went very still. He closed down. ~~Nothing stopped for him, not his mother's hysterical frustration, not the grim strangers striding all around him, not~~ 'Mary's Boy Child' looped inanely ~~looping on the mall tannoy. It all just went on around him as he~~. He absorbed this ~~blow, like a child on a street in the wake of a detonation;~~, deafened, stunned, eyes wide, the world blown open.

~~I stood up and walked over to them. I put my hand on the mother's shoulder. 'You need a break,' I said. 'You don't mean that. I know you don't. Here – let me take your little boy for a while and you have a break in that café there. Just sit in there and rest and I'll take him for a walk outside and find a tree somewhere and sit under it. Then later you can say sorry and go home and wrap up these presents together and put them under the tree. How does that sound?'~~

~~No, I didn't. Of course I didn't.~~ I caught my husband's eye ~~and knew he shared my unhappiness at being back in Australia, caught here in the very vortex of commercialism we both despised, witnessing something so miserable that it flooded us both with fresh misery.~~

~~I haven't mentioned my husband sitting there until now, but let me paint him into the scene now. I need this for context, for narrative, to make you understand why I didn't rise to my feet, propelled by righteous anger and a larger, calmer compassion, and approach that seething young woman at the very end of her tether. I looked over at him and for a second the~~. The notion of standing up and intervening hung between us~~, then I felt a wave of pure despair.~~. It held me in place like an undertow.

~~Believe me, I feel with you the narrative lockstep which now requires me to expand on this despair, to illustrate how this vignette is now progressing accordingly to mention that our marriage was teetering at that point, limping along on the baldest of tyres, almost out of gas. That we had no energy in ourselves to alleviate each other's misery, that we had lost the power and the will to do so. To turn this story to our endless true subject: myself. To make this~~ This boy and his mother were bit-players in a drama about a faltering marriage~~, to show how this moment was the all-important tipping point, then moving on to the Me Show~~ - the two of them nothing more than extras. ~~Catalysts. It's typical of life, I am sure you will agree, to provide us with our turning-point catalysts outside Kmart, to allow us to use others in this way.~~

Wait. I don't want to go there. I stood up. I walked over to the mother and her son. ~~The~~ In this other story the mother – somehow, implausibly, ~~I'll work on this part later –~~

allowed me to crouch down in front of her son, ignoring her, and speak to him.
'It's not *you,*' I said to the white-faced, trembling little boy. ~~'You're *fantastic*. Do you hear me? You're a great kid. Don't worry – your mum's under a lot of stress and adults say lots of crazy things they wish they hadn't said later. OK?~~ Remember what I'm telling you. It's not about you.'

No, I didn't. You know I didn't. The moment hung there, the chance to change the narrative. I assessed the energy and grief and courage it would require, to thresh and flounder against that debilitating undertow and stand up and do it.
~~I looked over at my husband, lost in~~ who would no longer be my husband only a few months from now. I noticed his ~~own~~ immobilising grief.
I'll tell you, although I don't need, nothing to ~~now, that the relationship crashed and burned a few short months later. It's enough that you know that I'm left~~do with this – ~~myself sitting, doing nothing, and that~~boy or his mother at all.

The boy would be eighteen now and I think of him all the time. I can tinker with the script all I like but this is the story I'm left with. Had I risen, I would have been the catalyst. I would have been someone else's turning point.
Had I risen, I wonder if I would even have had to write this now.

~~In Front of Kmart by Krissy Kneen~~

I was sitting on a plastic bench outside Kmart in a shopping mall. Five days before Christmas.

A young harassed mother near me was losing the plot with her young son.

The kid was about four, rattled, exhausted, as everyone else trudged around.

Christmas carol muzak swamped the air. The Kmart staff sported synthetic Santa hats, stony-faced, manhandling boxes across the registers.

'Listen to me!' she yelled, her face close to his. 'That's it! We're going home now, do you hear me?'

She shifted her massive plastic bags of Christmas shopping, gave him a good shake. The boy tried to direct his eyes somewhere else, out of the line of fire of her furious glare. Maybe she expected more resistance from him. Maybe she thought the idea of going home, far away from this wonderland of noise and toys, would make him cry and plead. She tightened her grip on his arm and shook him again.

'Santa's not coming,' she shouted. 'Santa hates you.'

The little boy went very still. He closed down.

'Mary's Boy Child' looped inanely. He absorbed this, deafened, stunned, eyes wide, the world blown open.

I caught my husband's eye. The notion of standing up and intervening hung between us. It held me in place like an undertow. This boy and his mother were bit-players in a drama about a faltering marriage – the two of them nothing more than extras.

I stood up. I walked over to the mother and her son. In this other story the mother – somehow, implausibly, allowed me to crouch down in front of her son, ignoring her, and speak to him.

'It's not you,' I said to the white-faced, trembling little boy. 'Remember what I'm telling you. It's not about you.'

The moment hung there, the chance to change the narrative. I assessed the energy and grief and courage it would require, to thresh and flounder against that debilitating undertow and stand up and do it.

I looked over at my husband who would no longer be my husband only a few months from now. I noticed his immobilising grief, nothing to do with this boy or his mother at all.

The boy would be eighteen now and I think of him all the time. I can tinker with the script all I like but this is the story I'm left with. Had I risen, I would have been the catalyst. I would have been someone else's turning point.

Had I risen, I wonder if I would even have had to write this now.

I was ~~sitting~~seated on a plastic bench outside Kmart in a shopping mall. Five days ~~before~~until Christmas.

A ~~young~~tired harassed mother near me was losing the plot with her young son.

The ~~kid~~boy was about four, rattled, exhausted, as everyone else trudging around. Christmas~~-carol~~ muzak swamped the air. The Kmart staff sported synthetic Santa hats, stony-faced, manhandling boxes across ~~the~~ registers.

'Listen to me~~!~~,' she yelled, her face close to his. 'That's it~~!~~. We're going home *now*, do you ~~hear~~understand me?'

She shifted her ~~massive~~humongous plastic bags of Christmas shopping, gave him a good shake. The boy tried to direct his ~~eyes~~gaze somewhere else, out of the line of fire of her furious glare. Maybe she ~~expected~~anticipated more resistance from him. Maybe she thought the idea of ~~going~~returning home, far away from this wonderland of noise and toys, would make him cry and plead. She tightened her grip on his arm and shook him~~-again~~.

'Santa's *not coming,*' she ~~shouted~~hissed.

'Santa *hates* you.'

The little boy went ~~very~~ still. He ~~closed~~withered down.

'Mary's Boy Child' ~~looped~~played inanely. He absorbed this, deafened, stunned, eyes wide, the world ~~blown~~wrenched open.

I caught my ~~husband's~~partner's eye. The ~~notion~~idea of standing up and intervening hung between us. It ~~held~~drowned me in place like an undertow. This boy and his mother were bit-players in a drama about a faltering marriage - the two of them ~~nothing~~no more than extras.

I stood~~-up~~. I walked ~~over~~ to the mother and her son. In this other story the mother~~–~~— somehow, implausibly, allowed me to crouch down in front of her son, ignoring her, and ~~speak~~bond to him.

'It's not *you,*' I said to the white-faced, trembling ~~little~~ boy. 'Remember what I'm telling you kid. It's not ~~about~~ you.'

The moment hung there, the chance to ~~change~~write the narrative. I assessed the energy and grief and courage it would ~~require~~take, to thresh and flounder against that debilitating undertow and stand up and do it.

I looked over at my husband who would no longer be my husband ~~only~~ a few months from now. I noticed his~~-immobilising~~ grief, nothing to do with this boy or his mother at all.

The boy would be eighteen by now and I think of him all the time. I can tinker with the sad script all I like but this is the story I'm left with. Had I risen then, I would have been the catalyst. I would have been someone else's chief turning point.

Had I risen, I wonder if I would ~~even~~ have had to write this now.

In Front of Myself by Robert Hoge

I was seated on a plastic bench outside Kmart in a shopping mall. Five days until Christmas.

A tired harassed mother near me was losing the plot with her young son.

The boy was about four, rattled, exhausted, as everyone else trudged around.

Christmas muzak swamped the air. The Kmart staff sported synthetic Santa hats, stony-faced, manhandling boxes across registers.

'Listen to me,' she yelled, her face close to his. 'That's it. We're going home now, do you understand me?'

She shifted her humongous plastic bags of Christmas shopping, gave him a good shake. The boy tried to direct his gaze somewhere else, out of the line of fire of her furious glare. Maybe she anticipated more resistance from him. Maybe she thought the idea of returning home, far away from this wonderland of noise and toys, would make him cry and plead. She tightened her grip on his arm and shook him.

'Santa's not coming,' she hissed. 'Santa hates you.'

The little boy went still. He withered down.

'Mary's Boy Child' played inanely. He absorbed this, deafened, stunned, eyes wide, the world wrenched open.

I caught my partner's eye. The idea of standing up and intervening hung between us. It drowned me in place like an undertow. This boy and his mother were bit-players in a drama about a faltering marriage - the two of them no more than extras.

I stood. I walked to the mother and her son. In this other story the mother – somehow, implausibly, allowed me to crouch down in front of her son, ignoring her, and bond to him.

'It's not you,' I said to the white-faced, trembling boy. 'Remember what I'm telling you kid. It's not you.'

The moment hung there, the chance to write the narrative. I assessed the energy and grief and courage it would take, to thresh and flounder against that debilitating undertow and stand up and do it.

I looked over at my husband who would no longer be my husband a few months from now. I noticed his grief, nothing to do with this boy or his mother at all.

The boy would be eighteen by now and I think of him all the time. I can tinker with the sad script all I like but this is the story I'm left with. Had I risen then, I would have been the catalyst. I would have been someone else's chief turning point.

Had I risen, I wonder if I would have had to write this now.

I was~~We were~~ seated on a plastic bench outside Kmart in a shopping mall. Five days until Christmas.

~~A tired harassed mother near me was losing the plot with her young son.~~

The boy was about ~~four~~three, rattled, exhausted, as everyone else trudging around. Christmas muzak swamped the air. The Kmart staff sported synthetic Santa hats, stony-faced, manhandling boxes across registers.

'Listen to me,' she yelled, her face close to his. 'That's it. We're going home *now*, do you understand me?'

She shifted her humongous plastic bags of Christmas shopping, gave him a good shake. The boy tried to direct his gaze somewhere else, out of the line of fire of her furious glare. Maybe she anticipated more resistance from him. Maybe she thought the idea of returning home, far away from this wonderland of noise and toys, would make him cry and plead. She tightened her grip on his arm and shook him.

'Santa's *not coming*,' she hissed. 'Santa *hates* you.'

The little boy went still. He withered down. 'Mary's Boy Child' played inanely. He absorbed this, deafened, stunned, eyes wide, the world wrenched open.

I caught my partner's eye. The idea of standing up and intervening hung between us. ~~It drowned me in place~~I felt like ~~an undertow.~~a swimmer in a rip. This boy and his mother were bit-players in a drama about a faltering marriage~~—~~—the two of them no more than extras. Our private drama was so all-consuming that everyone else got driven out of the picture or relegated to a walk-on part. Or that's how it felt at the time. As it turned out, the boy and his mother were much more than that.

I stood~~. I~~ and walked to over the mother and her son. ~~In this other story~~ I barely glanced at the mother~~—somehow, implausibly, allowed me~~, only enough to ~~crouch~~register that she was so stunned by my sudden appearance that she was waiting to see what came next. I crouched down in front of her ~~son, ignoring her, and bond to him.~~white-faced, trembling son.

'It's not *you*,' I said to ~~the white faced, trembling boy.~~him. 'Remember what I'm telling you kid. It's not you.'

~~The moment hung there, the chance to write the narrative. I assessed the energy and grief and courage it would take, to thresh and flounder against that debilitating undertow and stand up and do it.~~

~~I looked over at my husband who would no longer be my husband a few months from now. I noticed his grief, nothing to do with this boy or his mother at all.~~

~~The boy would be eighteen by now and I think of him all the time. I can tinker with the sad script all I like but this is the story I'm left with. Had I risen then, I would have been the catalyst. I would have been someone else's chief turning point.~~

~~Had I risen, I wonder if I would have had to write this now.~~

I thought I was making a difference in the boy's life, helping him see it wasn't his fault. But even then I think I knew that I wasn't really doing it for him. I was doing it for me. In that boy I saw my young self, cowed and battered by my mother's unpredictable moods and hair-trigger temper.

As I stood up again, the mother stepped towards me. I had never seen someone go purple with rage before. I had read about it in books but never seen it. She put her face right up to mine.

'What the fuck do you think you're doing? This is none of your bloody fuckin' business, you interfering goody-goody.'

By this time, my wife had come up behind me. I saw the mother's eyes swoop on her, as if she was going to give my wife a piece of her mind, too.

Helena touched me on the shoulder. 'There's nothing more you can do, Jay.'

I nodded to the boy, whose eyes were almost popping out of his head as they flicked from me to his mother to my wife and back again. I like to think that when his eyes met mine the second time around, he gave a small nod. That he had absorbed and understood what I said, or that he would at a later date. As we walked away, I said as much to Helena. She said she hoped so, too, although she suspected the boy was too young. Who remembered anything much from when they were three?

I didn't realise how worked up I was until I caught myself almost losing it with Helena, right there, out the front of Kmart, with Christmas shoppers all around us. I couldn't look at her. Why did she have to say such incredibly stupid things? It didn't matter if the boy didn't remember. What mattered was that he didn't blame himself. She was implying that what I done hadn't been worth it. How fucking dare she? At least I didn't sit back, like she did, and leave the boy to his fate.

It was all boiling around inside me, about to come gushing out like black sludge from deep underground, when I somehow stopped myself. She wasn't denying it, she was just being realistic. The more important question was why I had over-reacted again. Why I was always hitting the roof over seeming little things? No prizes for guessing where that came from. The problem was that nothing ever felt small to me. Everything felt big, the way it does when you're a kid. Every time I lost it with my wife I was four again, or five or six, bewildered by the way my mother was behaving and unable to make anything change.

But on this particular day, I realised things could change. I could change. And in that moment I felt more in command of myself than I had for as long as I can remember. That mother and boy weren't bit players, they weren't extras. They were my childhood come back to haunt me. And for once, I didn't fume and feel helpless and then take it out on my wife. I would never know whether or not my intervention made any difference in that boy's life. But I knew, without a moment's doubt, that it made all the difference in mine.

~~In Front of Myself by Fiona Capp~~

We were seated on a plastic bench outside Kmart in a shopping mall. Five days until Christmas.

A tired harassed mother near me was losing the plot with her young son. The boy was about three, rattled, exhausted, as everyone else trudging around.

Christmas muzak swamped the air. The Kmart staff sported synthetic Santa hats, stony-faced, manhandling boxes across registers.

'Listen to me,' she yelled, her face close to his. 'That's it. We're going home now, do you understand me?'

She shifted her humongous plastic bags of Christmas shopping, gave him a good shake. The boy tried to direct his gaze somewhere else, out of the line of fire of her furious glare. Maybe she anticipated more resistance from him. Maybe she thought the idea of returning home, far away from this wonderland of noise and toys, would make him cry and plead. She tightened her grip on his arm and shook him.

'Santa's not coming,' she hissed. 'Santa hates you.'

The little boy went still. He withered down.

'Mary's Boy Child' played inanely. He absorbed this, deafened, stunned, eyes wide, the world wrenched open.

I caught my partner's eye. The idea of standing up and intervening hung between us. I felt like a swimmer in a rip. This boy and his mother were bit-players in a drama about a faltering marriage – the two of them no more than extras. Our private drama was so all-consuming that everyone else got driven out of the picture or relegated to a walk-on part. Or that's how it felt at the time. As it turned out, the boy and his mother were much more than that.

I stood and walked to over the mother and her son. I barely glanced at the mother, only enough to register that she was so stunned by my sudden appearance that she was waiting to see what came next. I crouched down in front of her white-faced, trembling son.

'It's not you,' I said to him. 'Remember what I'm telling you kid. It's not you.'

I thought I was making a difference in the boy's life, helping him see it wasn't his fault. But even then I think I knew that I wasn't really doing it for him. I was doing it for me. In that boy I saw my young self, cowed and battered by my mother's unpredictable moods and hair-trigger temper.

As I stood up again, the mother stepped towards me. I had never seen someone go purple with rage before. I had read about it in books but never seen it. She put her face right up to mine.

'What the fuck do you think you're doing? This is none of your bloody fuckin' business, you interfering goody-goody.'

By this time, my wife had come up behind me. I saw the mother's eyes swoop on her, as if she was going to give my wife a piece of her mind, too.

Helena touched me on the shoulder. 'There's nothing more you can do, Jay.'

I nodded to the boy, whose eyes were almost popping out of his head as they flicked from me to his mother to my wife and back again.

I like to think that when his eyes met mine the second time around, he gave a small nod. That he had absorbed and understood what I said, or that he would at a later date. As we walked away, I said as much to Helena. She said she hoped so, too, although she suspected the boy was too young. Who remembered anything much from when they were three?

I didn't realise how worked up I was until I caught myself almost losing it with Helena, right there, out the front of Kmart, with Christmas shoppers all around us. I couldn't look at her. Why did she have to say such incredibly stupid things? It didn't matter if the boy didn't remember. What mattered was that he didn't blame himself. She was implying that what I had done hadn't been worth it. How fucking dare she? At least I didn't sit back, like she did, and leave the boy to his fate.

It was all boiling around inside me, about to come gushing out like black sludge from deep underground, when I somehow stopped myself. She wasn't denying it, she was just being realistic. The more important question was why I had over-reacted again. Why I was always hitting the roof over seeming little things? No prizes for guessing where that came from. The problem was that nothing ever felt small to me. Everything felt big, the way it does when you're a kid. Every time I lost it with my wife I was four again, or five or six, bewildered by the way my mother was behaving and unable to make anything change.

But on this particular day, I realised things could change. I could change. And in that moment I felt more in command of myself than I had for as long as I can remember.

That mother and boy weren't bit players, they weren't extras. They were my childhood come back to haunt me. And for once, I didn't fume and feel helpless and then take it out on my wife. I would never know whether or not my intervention made any difference in that boy's life. But I knew, without a moment's doubt, that it made all the difference in mine.

We were seated on a plastic bench outside Kmart in a shopping mall. Five days until Christmas.

A tired harassed mother near me was losing the plot with her young son. The boy was about three, rattled, exhausted, as everyone else trudging around.

Christmas muzak swamped the air. The Kmart staff sported synthetic Santa hats, stony-faced, manhandling boxes across registers.

'Listen to me,' she yelled, her face close to his. 'That's it. We're going home *now*, do you understand me?'

She shifted her humongous plastic bags of Christmas shopping, gave him a good shake. The boy tried to direct his gaze somewhere else, out of the line of fire of her furious glare. Maybe she anticipated more resistance from him. Maybe she thought the idea of returning home, far away from this wonderland of noise and toys, would make him cry and plead. She tightened her grip on his arm and shook him.

'Santa's *not coming*,' she hissed. 'Santa *hates* you.'

The little boy went still. He withered down.

'Mary's Boy Child' played inanely. He absorbed this, deafened, stunned, eyes wide, the world wrenched open.

I caught my partner's eye. The idea of standing up and intervening hung between us. I felt like a swimmer in a rip. This boy and his mother were bit-players in a drama about a faltering marriage—the two of them no more than extras. Our private drama was so all-consuming that everyone else got driven out of the picture or relegated to a walk-on part. Or that's how it felt at the time. As it turned out, the boy and his mother were much more than that.

I stood and walked to over the mother and her son. I barely glanced at the mother, only enough to register that she was so stunned by my sudden appearance that she was waiting to see what came next. I crouched down in front of her white-faced, trembling son.

'It's not *you*,' I said to him. 'Remember what I'm telling you kid. It's not you.'

I thought I was making a difference in the boy's life, helping him see it wasn't his fault. But even then I think I knew that I wasn't really doing it for him. I was doing it for me. In that boy I saw my young self, cowed and battered by my mother's unpredictable moods and hair-trigger temper.

As I stood up again, the mother stepped towards me. I had never seen someone go purple with rage before. I had read about it in books but never seen it. She put her face right up to mine.

'What the fuck do you think you're doing? This is none of your bloody fuckin' business, you interfering goody-goody.'

By this time, my wife had come up behind me. I saw the mother's eyes swoop on her, as if she was going to give my wife a piece of her mind, too.

Helena touched me on the shoulder. 'There's nothing more you can do, Jay.'

I nodded to the boy, whose eyes were almost popping out of his head as they flicked from me to his mother to my wife and back again.

I like to think that when his eyes met mine the second time around, he gave a small nod. That he had absorbed and understood what I said, or that he would at a later date. As we walked away, I said as much to Helena. She said she hoped so, too, although she suspected the boy was too young. Who remembered anything much from when they were three?

I didn't realise how worked up I was until I caught myself almost losing it with Helena, right there, out the front of Kmart, with Christmas shoppers all around us. I couldn't look at her. Why did she have to say such incredibly stupid things? It didn't matter if the boy didn't remember. What mattered was that he didn't blame himself. She was implying that what I done hadn't been worth it. How fucking dare she? At least I didn't sit back, like she did, and leave the boy to his fate.

It was all boiling around inside me, about to come gushing out like black sludge from deep underground, when I somehow stopped myself. She wasn't denying it, she was just being realistic. The more important question was why I had over-reacted again. Why I was always hitting the roof over seeming little things? No prizes for guessing where that came from. The problem was that nothing ever felt small to me. Everything felt big, the way it does when you're a kid. Every time I lost it with my wife I was four again, or five or six, bewildered by the way my mother was behaving and unable to make anything change.

But on this particular day, I realised things could change. I could change. And in that moment I felt more in command of myself than I had for as long as I can remember.

That mother and boy weren't bit players, they weren't extras. They were my childhood come back to haunt me. And for once, I didn't fume and feel helpless and then take it out on my wife. I would never know whether or not my

~~intervention made any difference in that boy's life. But I knew, without a moment's doubt, that it made all the difference in mine.~~

Welcome to AusStories v2.6

Congratulations on purchasing AusStories v2.6!

In just a few moments, you'll be writing your very own Australian masterpiece with the help of the AusStories database, which contains over nine hundred million possible novels, short stories, essays and poems.

Before we start, please take some time to setup the program for optimal experience.

Setup

Three upgrades have been detected for AusStories v2.6

Do you want to upgrade to AusStories v2.6BasicWinton for just $4.99?

Features include:

- 750,000 + ways to describe the surf.
- Over 500 damaged male characters to choose from.
- A magical realism patch.
- Guaranteed shortlisting for the Miles Franklin Award.

Do you want to upgrade to AusStories v2.6PremiumWhite for just $9.99?

Features include:

- Exclusive Greek and European settings, as well as detailed, lyrical descriptions of the bush and the town of 'Sarsaparilla.'
- High Modernism find and replace function (All two-syllable words are substituted for four-syllable synonyms).
- Dun-coloured journalistic realism detector.

Do you want to upgrade to AusStories v2.6SuperpremiumMurnane for just $149.99?

Features include:

- One handed typing option.
- Automatic removal of any distinguishing traits from characters.
- Plot minimiser.
- Journal to record bowel movements in exhaustive detail.

You have not chosen to upgrade AusStoriesv2.6 at this time.

Thank you for completing setup.

AusStories v2.6: Let's Get Writing!

What form would you like to write in?

Essay
Poetry
Novella
Short Story ✓
Novel

You have chosen: short story.

What genre would you like your short story to be?

Horror Fantasy
Metafiction
Legend Tall Tale
Yarn Humorous
Mystery
Crime
Satire
Apocalyptic Campus
Experimental
Steampunk Thriller
Literary realism (default) ✓ science-fiction
Gothic
Erotic Western
Weird
War
Adventure Ghost

1 2 3….25

You have chosen literary realism (default).

AusStories V2.6 offers over 300 different genres to work in. Are you sure?

Y

You have chosen literary realism (default).

Choose a setting.

Bush
Beach
City ✓

You have chosen 'city.'

Please select from the following sub-menu. More than one option can be chosen.

Police station
Hospital
Kitchen
Dentist
Office
Kmart ✓
Factory
School
Park

You have chosen 'Kmart.'

~~Welcome to AusStories v2.6 by Ryan O'Neill~~

Congratulations on purchasing AusStories v2.6!

In just a few moments, you'll be writing your very own Australian masterpiece with the help of the AusStories database, which contains over nine hundred million possible novels, short stories, essays and poems.

Before we start, please take some time to setup the program for optimal experience.

Setup

Do you want to upgrade to AusStories v2.6BasicWinton for just $4.99?

Features include:

- 750,000 + ways to describe the surf.
- Over 500 damaged male characters to choose from.
- A magical realism patch.
- Guaranteed shortlisting for the Miles Franklin Award.

Do you want to upgrade to AusStories v2.6PremiumWhite for just $9.99?

Features include:

- Exclusive Greek and European settings, as well as detailed, lyrical descriptions of the bush and the town of 'Sarsaparilla.'
- High Modernism find and replace function (All two-syllable words are substituted for four-syllable synonyms).
- Dun-coloured journalistic realism detector.

Do you want to upgrade to AusStories v2.6SuperpremiumMurnane for just $149.99?

Features include:

- One handed typing option.
- Automatic removal of any distinguishing traits from characters.
- Plot minimiser.
- Journal to record bowel movements in exhaustive detail.

You have not chosen to upgrade AusStoriesv2.6 at this time.
Thank you for completing setup.

AusStories v2.6: Let's Get Writing!

What form would you like to write in?

- Essay
- Poetry
- Novella
- **Short story ✓**
- Novel

You have chosen: Short story.

What genre would you like your short story to be?

- Horror
- Fantasy
- Metafiction
- Legend
- Tall Tale
- Yarn
- Humorous
- Mystery
- Satire
- Apocalyptic
- Campus
- Experimental
- Steampunk
- Thriller
- **Literary realism (default) ✓**
- Crime
- Science-fiction
- Gothic
- Erotic Western
- Weird
- War
- Adventure
- Ghost

1 2 3...25

You have chosen: Literary realism (default).
AusStories V2.6 offers over 300 different genres to work in. Are you sure?

Y

You have chosen: Literary realism (default).

Choose a setting.

- Bush
- Beach
- **City ✓**

You have chosen: City.

Please select from the following sub-menu.
More than one option can be chosen.

- Police station
- Hospital
- Kitchen
- Dentist
- Office
- **Kmart ✓**
- Factory
- School
- Park

You have chosen: Kmart.

Input a time for the story to take place.
Time determines some of the default themes of the story e.g. Easter = death and rebirth. New Year's Eve = new beginnings etc)

You have chosen: December 24th at 3pm.

Please choose from the following narrative modes.

- **1st Person ✓**

- 2nd Person (Advanced Users Only)
- 3rd Person Omniscient
- 3rd Person Limited
- 1st Person Plural (Advanced Users Only)

You have chosen: 1st Person.

Choose a tense.

- **Present ✓**
- Past

In order to determine the length of the story,
please select from one of the following forms:

- **The Josephine Rowe (less than 1000 words)** ✓
- The Cate Kennedy (3000 words)
- The Nam Le (10,000 words)
- The David Malouf (15,000 + words)

You have chosen: The Josephine Rowe.

Choose additional themes (maximum five)
from the list below.

'Forgiveness' and 'Hope' are mandatory for stories set on Christmas Eve.

- **Parental love ✓**
- **Childhood ✓**
- Nature
- Communication
- Books
- Disillusionment

- **Love ✓**
- Death
- **Memory ✓**
- Capitalism
- **Marriage ✓**
- Heroism
- Temptation
- Pride

1 2 3……..…………………………………135

Choose your preferred form of imagery

- Metaphor
- **Simile ✓**

You have chosen 'simile.'

Select similes (minimum two) from the list.

- **Like a swimmer in a rip ✓**
- Like a cat on a hot tin roof
- Like a candle in the wind
- Like a shag on a rock
- **Like black sludge from deep underground ✓**
- Like a dog with its bone
- As white as snow
- As pretty as a picture

1 2 3…..……………………………………948

Choose from one of the seven plots below.

- From poverty to wealth
- The mission
- Rebirth
- **Defeating the monster ✓**
- Comedy
- Tragedy
- Departure and arrival

Input the number of flat and round characters to feature in the story.

Round: **1**

Flat: **3**

Choose from the following plot points to complete the structure of the story.

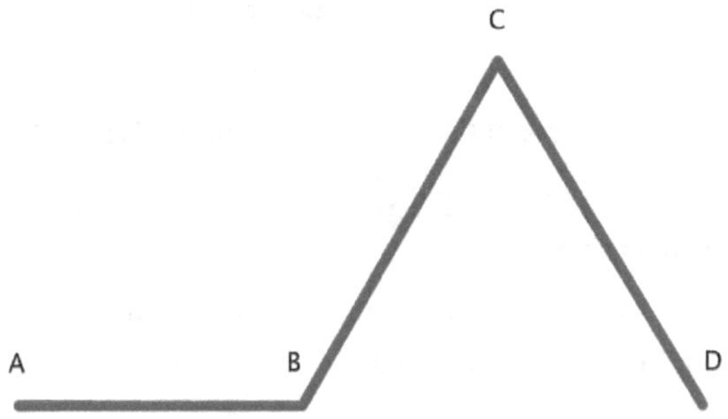

A for Exposition

- A woman's husband has just left her on Christmas Eve.
- A Kmart employee is working on Christmas Eve.
- A mother spends Christmas Eve searching everywhere for a special toy for her child.
- **A husband and wife are Christmas shopping. ✓**

B for Conflict

- He spots a shoplifter and gives chase.
- She tries to grab the last toy from the shelf, but another woman has seen it.
- The woman snaps and shouts at her son.
- **The husband sees a woman shouting at her son and intervenes. ✓**

C for Climax

- The woman pushes at the other shopper, who hits her head on the floor and dies.
- **The husband tells the boy it is not his fault. ✓**
- He catches the shoplifter, realises she is an ex-girlfriend and lets her go.
- The woman is shamed and humiliated by the intervention of a bystander.

D for Resolution

- The woman spends Christmas in prison, awaiting trial for manslaughter.

- The thief blackmails the man for letting her off, and he pays her $100 not to tell his supervisor.
- The woman is left weeping and broken as her son tries to comfort her.
- **The husband reflects on his own childhood. ✓**

Do you want the story to conclude with a moment of epiphany? (Recommended)

- **Yes ✓**
- No

Choose one of the following titles

- In Front of Kmart
- Cyclone Dragitsa
- Things We Didn't See Coming in Front of Us
- My Father as a Short Story
- Beside Myself
- I'm not OKmart
- Kmart Behind Me
- **In Front of Myself ✓**
- Walking the Walk
- Me, Myself and I
- The Accident

Thank you for using AusStories v2.6. When you are ready to write your story, press Start.

..........LOADING.........

~~The Accident by Fiona Capp~~

I wish I could say that it didn't happen. I wish I could say that I wasn't there. Above all, I wish I could change the way events unfolded so that the cyclist took another route or that the truck came down the hill long before the cyclist, or that the road had been wider. Or, or, or. Three wishes that I will never be granted. But I like to think that someone else will.

It was approaching peak hour on an overcast afternoon. I was on my way to a tutorial, thinking about the preparation I should have done. At the end of my street was a main road with no traffic lights. Getting out into the busy thoroughfare, with cars and trucks hurtling down the hill and over the bridge across the freeway, was always difficult. Watching it all flash by, I noticed a cyclist cruising down the far, outside lane. He was wearing a back pack. A semi-trailer passed him, blocking my view. Then I saw a grey bundle caught up in the big wheels of the semi. It looked like a kind of sack.

On the footpath on my side of the road were two teenage boys. They were laughing because they could not believe their eyes. They were laughing out of horror. At first the driver of the semi didn't appear to realise what had happened. A hundred metres up the road he finally stopped. Scattered behind his vehicle was a trail of what looked like intestines. Then I saw part of a body without a head. Inside the bubble of my car I was whispering, 'No! No!' What I was most aware of was the fraudulence of suburbia, its illusion of safety and security. I could not go to my tutorial. I turned the car around and drove back home. On the way I saw the man from the flat above me driving towards the intersection. I wanted to tell him to go back but didn't know how.

When I got back to the flat, I didn't know what to do with myself. I sat in the big armchair. I walked around the lounge room. I stared out the window. I needed to tell someone what I had witnessed but my partner wasn't home. The urge was so strong I rang my parents. As I spoke, I still hoped that I might have got it wrong. People get 'run over' or 'hit by a car'. No one told me that they get disembowelled or ripped apart. Perhaps I had led too sheltered a life. I was still in my twenties and I wanted my parents to tell me these things can't happen. Don't happen. All they could do was say was how awful it was. My mother, who is a psychologist, suggested that I get professional help to deal with the shock of what I had seen. I was indignant. Why did I need help? I was the lucky bystander. I was still alive. It was the cyclist's parents or wife or children who would need help. Not me.

As I hung the phone up I saw Barry, the drug dealer from upstairs coming up the front path. His face was puffy and he was swearing to himself, which was nothing unusual, except that I knew what he had seen. I had no desire to talk to him. He went upstairs and I heard muffled, urgent conversation. A few minutes later, he was heading out again with his girlfriend.

Car doors slammed and an engine started up. I raced outside to see them disappearing up the street toward the intersection where it happened. Shock gave way to anger. I shouted after them but they couldn't hear me. I was still on the footpath out the front of the flats when, some minutes later, their car reappeared having done the block and was about to turn back into the street. I waited, ready to give Barry a piece of my mind. But instead of turning right, he turned left and headed back to the intersection for a second look.

When I heard the knock on the door I knew who it was. It wasn't enough that he had had three viewings himself and had shown his girlfriend the remains. Now he wanted to 'share' it with us, too. I could imagine him standing in the hallway, shuffling on the spot, his shoulders hunched. I opened the door.

Barry looked at me warily. He really wanted to speak to my partner. I told him my partner wasn't home but that didn't stop him. He had something to report and like the Ancient Mariner, he was compelled to speak.

'You should've seen what happened up there.' He waved his arm in the direction of the intersection. 'This horrible accident –'

Normally I listened to his rambles, half annoyed, half intrigued by the unexpected things he came out with. But this time, I didn't let him finish.

'You fucking vulture.'

I told him I was there when it happened and that I saw him take Annie for a look. I told him that no one in their right mind would show someone else.

'Hey, hey,' he began in his cool-it voice. 'She rides a bike, right? I wanted her to see what can happen.' He said that Annie was often reckless. It wasn't enough to tell her about it. He wanted to show her something she wouldn't forget. Annie was crazier than he was, so I could believe she would be reckless on her bike. But she wasn't thick. The reported details were terrible enough to scare anyone.

Later on that evening, there was a tentative knock at the door. It was Barry again. He apologised for upsetting me and handed me two valium tablets in a foil wrapper. He said they would help me sleep.

Dumbfounded, I took them from him. I told myself he meant well. A drug-dealer with drugs for every occasion. I muttered 'thanks' and quickly closed the door. I looked down at the tablets in my palm.

Maybe I did need help.

~~The Accident~~

~~I wish I could say that it~~ Crash

It didn't happen. ~~I wish I could say that~~ I wasn't there. ~~Above all, I wish I could~~I can change the ~~way~~ events ~~unfolded so that the~~ unfold their unfolding. The cyclist ~~took~~takes another route ~~or that~~; the truck ~~came~~comes down the hill long before the ~~cyclist, or that the~~bike. The road ~~had been~~is wider. Or, or, or. Three wishes. That's all I need. Three wishes that I ~~will~~may never be granted. But if not me, I like to think that someone else will.

~~It was approaching peak~~Peak hour ~~on an~~. An overcast afternoon. I was on my way to a tutorial, thinking about the preparation I should have done but hadn't. At the end of my street was a main road with no traffic lights. Getting ~~out into~~onto the busy thoroughfare, with cars and trucks hurtling down the hill and over the bridge across the freeway, was always difficult. Watching it ~~all~~ flash by, I noticed a cyclist cruising down the far, outside lane. He was wearing a ~~back pack~~backpack. A semi-trailer passed ~~him~~, blocking my view. Then I saw a grey bundle caught up in the big wheels of the semi. It looked like a ~~kind of sack~~ sack of potatoes – rolling between the wheels..

On the footpath on my side of the road were two teenage boys. They were ~~laughing~~crying because they could not believe their eyes. They were ~~laughing~~crying out of shock, out of horror. At first the driver of the semi didn't appear to realise what had happened. A hundred metres up the road he finally stopped. Scattered behind his vehicle was a trail of what looked like intestines. Then ~~I saw~~, part of a body without a head. ~~Inside~~Next a patch of skin.

There was a whispering coming from inside the bubble of my car ~~I was whispering~~:; 'No! ~~No!'~~, no, no.' Then I became aware that the whispering was coming from me. What I was most aware of though, was the fraudulence of suburbia, its illusion of safety and security. I could not go to my tutorial.

I turned the car around and drove ~~back~~ home. On the way I saw the man from the flat above me driving towards the intersection. I wanted to tell him to go back ~~but didn't know how~~; to save himself but mostly to save me. A horror witnessed by someone you know is not to be denied.

When I got back to the flat, I didn't know what to do ~~with myself~~. I poured a glass of reds wine then shoved it away. I sat in the big armchair ~~,~~ – the one that felt like it was giving me a hug but it felt like I was being smothered. I walked around the lounge room. I stared out the window ~~,~~ but the flashing lights I needed to tell someone what ~~I had~~I'd witnessed but my partner wasn't home. The urge was so strong I rang my parents. As I spoke, I still hoped that I might have got it wrong. People get 'run over' or 'hit by a car'. No one told me that they get disembowelled or ripped apart. Perhaps I ~~had~~ led too sheltered a life. I was still in my twenties and I wanted my parents to tell me that these things can't happen ~~.~~, that the universe forbids it. Don't happen. All they could do was say was how awful it was. My mother, ~~who is~~ a psychologist, suggested that I get professional help to deal with the shock of what I had seen. I was indignant. Why did *I* need help? I was the lucky bystander. I was still alive. It was the cyclist's parents or wife or children who would need help. ~~Not me.~~

~~As~~ I hung ~~the phone~~ up ~~I~~and saw Barry, the drug dealer from upstairs coming up the front path. His face was puffy and he was swearing to himself, which was nothing unusual, except ~~that~~ I knew what he had seen. I had no desire to talk to him. He went upstairs and I heard muffled, urgent conversation. A few minutes later, he was heading out again with his girlfriend.

Car doors slammed and an engine started ~~up~~. I raced outside to see them disappearing ~~up the street~~ toward the intersection ~~where it happened. Shock gave way to anger.~~. Anger washed over my shock. I shouted after them but ~~they couldn't hear me~~only my ears heard. I was still on the footpath out the front of the flats when, some minutes later, their car reappeared having done the block and was about to turn back into the street. I waited, ready to give Barry a piece of my mind. But instead of turning right, he ~~turned left and~~ headed back to the intersection for a second look.

When I heard the knock ~~on the door~~ I knew who it was. It wasn't enough ~~that~~ he had had three viewings ~~himself~~ and had shown his girlfriend the remains. Now he wanted to 'share' it with us, too. I could imagine him standing in the hallway, shuffling on the spot, his shoulders hunched. I opened the door.

Barry looked at me warily. He really wanted to speak to my partner. I told him my partner wasn't home but that didn't stop him. He had something important to report and like the Ancient Mariner, he was compelled to speak. And to me it was.

'You should've seen what happened up ~~there~~the road.' He waved his arm in the direction of the intersection. ~~'This horrible accident~~'Gruesome –'

Normally I listened to his rambles, half annoyed, half intrigued by the unexpected things he came out with. ~~But this~~This time, I didn't let him finish.

'~~You fucking~~Fucking vulture.'

~~I told him~~ 'I was there ~~when~~,' I said. 'When he… When it happened ~~and that~~. I saw ~~him~~you take Annie for a look. ~~I told him that no one in their right mind~~Why would ~~*show*~~you *take* someone else ~~.~~ there? To *show* them?'

'Hey, hey,' he began in his cool-it voice. 'She rides a bike, right? I wanted her to see what can happen.'

He said ~~that~~ Annie was often reckless. It wasn't enough to tell her about it. He wanted to show her something she wouldn't forget.

Annie was crazier than he was, so I could believe she would be reckless on her bike. But she wasn't thick. The reported details ~~were~~should be terrible enough to scare anyone.

Later ~~on~~ that evening, there was a tentative knock at the door. ~~It was~~ Barry again. He apologised for upsetting me and handed me two ~~valium~~Valium tablets in ~~a~~ foil ~~wrapper~~. He said they would help me sleep.

Dumbfounded, I took them from him. I told myself he meant well. A drug-dealer with drugs for every occasion. I muttered 'thanks' and quickly closed the door. I looked down at the tablets in my palm.

~~Maybe~~ I ~~did need help~~wished to sleep.

And this one was granted.

But not without dreams. Of wheels and skin.

And the punctuated pieces of a person, spread across bitumen.

~~Crash by Robert Hoge~~

It didn't happen. I wasn't there. I can change the events – unfold their unfolding. The cyclist takes another route; the truck comes down the hill long before the bike. The road is wider. Or, or, or. Three wishes. That's all I need. Three wishes that I may never be granted. But if not me, I like to think that someone else will.

Peak hour. An overcast afternoon. I was on my way to a tutorial, thinking about the preparation I should have done but hadn't. At the end of my street was a main road with no traffic lights. Getting onto the busy thoroughfare, with cars and trucks hurtling down the hill and over the bridge across the freeway, was always difficult. Watching it flash by, I noticed a cyclist cruising down the far, outside lane. He was wearing a backpack. A semi-trailer passed, blocking my view. Then I saw a grey bundle caught up in the big wheels of the semi. It looked like a sack of potatoes – rolling between the wheels..

On the footpath on my side of the road were two teenage boys. They were crying because they could not believe their eyes. They were crying out of shock, out of horror. At first the driver of the semi didn't appear to realise what had happened. A hundred metres up the road he finally stopped. Scattered behind his vehicle was a trail of what looked like intestines. Then, part of a body without a head. Next a patch of skin.

There was a whispering coming from inside the bubble of my car: 'No, no, no.' Then I became aware that the whispering was coming from me. What I was most aware of though, was the fraudulence of suburbia, its illusion of safety and security. I could not go to my tutorial.

I turned the car around and drove home. On the way I saw the man from the flat above me driving towards the intersection. I wanted to tell him to go back; to save himself but mostly to save me. A horror witnessed by someone you know is not to be denied.

When I got back to the flat, I didn't know what to do. I poured a glass of red wine then shoved it away. I sat in the big armchair – the one that felt like it was giving me a hug but it felt like I was being smothered. I walked around the lounge room. I stared out the window at the flashing lights

I needed to tell someone what I'd witnessed but my partner wasn't home. The urge was so strong I rang my parents. As I spoke, I still hoped that I might have got it wrong. People get 'run over' or 'hit by a car'. No one told me that they get disembowelled or ripped apart. Perhaps I led too sheltered a life. I was still in my twenties and I wanted my parents to tell me that these things can't happen, that the universe forbids it. Don't happen. All they could do was say was how awful it was. My mother, a psychologist, suggested that I get professional help to deal with the shock of what I had seen. I was indignant. Why did I need help? I was the lucky bystander. I was still alive. It was the cyclist's parents or wife or children who would need help.

I hung up and saw Barry, the drug dealer from upstairs coming up the front path. His face was puffy and he was swearing to himself, which was nothing unusual, except I knew what he had seen. I had no desire to talk to him. He went upstairs and I heard muffled, urgent conversation. A few minutes later, he was heading out again with his girlfriend.

Car doors slammed and an engine started. I raced outside to see them disappearing toward the intersection. Anger washed over my shock. I shouted after them but only my ears heard. I was still on the footpath out the front of the flats when, some minutes later, their car reappeared having done the block and was about to turn back into the street. I waited, ready to give Barry a piece of my mind. But instead of turning right, he headed back to the intersection for a second look.

When I heard the knock I knew who it was. It wasn't enough he had had three viewings and had shown his girlfriend the remains. Now he wanted to 'share' it with us, too. I could imagine him standing in the hallway, shuffling on the spot, his shoulders hunched. I opened the door.

Barry looked at me warily. He really wanted to speak to my partner. I told him my partner wasn't home but that didn't stop him. He had something important to report and like the Ancient Mariner, he was compelled to speak. And to me it was.

'You should've seen what happened up the road.' He waved his arm in the direction of the intersection. 'Gruesome –'

Normally I listened to his rambles, half annoyed, half intrigued by the unexpected things he came out with. This time, I didn't let him finish.

'Fucking vulture. I was there,' I said. 'When he… When it happened. I saw you take Annie for a look. Why would you take someone else there? To show them?'

'Hey, hey,' he began in his cool-it voice. 'She rides a bike, right? I wanted her to see what can happen.'

He said Annie was often reckless. It wasn't enough to tell her about it. He wanted to show her something she wouldn't forget. Annie was crazier than he was, so I could believe she would be reckless on her bike. But she wasn't thick. The reported details should be terrible enough to scare anyone.

Later that evening, there was a tentative knock at the door. Barry again. He apologised for upsetting me and handed me two Valium tablets in foil. He said they would help me sleep.

Dumbfounded, I took them from him. I told myself he meant well. A drug-dealer with drugs for every occasion. I muttered 'thanks' and quickly closed the door. I looked down at the tablets in my palm.

I wished to sleep.

And this one was granted.

But not without dreams. Of wheels and skin. And the punctuated pieces of a person, spread across bitumen.

~~*It didn't happen. I wasn't there. I can change the events – unfold their unfolding. The cyclist takes another route; the truck comes down the hill long before the bike. The road is wider. Or, or, or. Three wishes. That's all I need. Three wishes that I may never be granted. But if not me, I like to think that someone else will.*~~

~~Peak hour. An overcast afternoon. I was on my way to a tutorial, thinking about the preparation I should have done but hadn't. At the end of my~~Twenty-Five Things I am Prepared to Talk About Other Than What You Want Me to Talk About

1. It was peak hour, and the afternoon was overcast. There was a breeze coming from the southeast, and the temperature was, according to the newspaper, twenty-two degrees. The UV index was- Yes, all that is important, but fine. I'll go on.

2. I was driving to uni with T.S. Eliot, Ted Hughes and W.H. Auden piled onto the passenger seat. There was a tutorial on Auden's Musée des Beux Arts at ten o'clock, and I wanted to get there early, because I hadn't read it.

3. At the end of the street was a main road with no traffic lights. Getting onto the busy thoroughfare, with cars and trucks hurtling down the hill and over the bridge across the freeway, was always difficult. ~~Watching it flash by, I noticed a cyclist cruising down the far, outside lane. He was wearing a backpack. A semi-trailer passed, blocking my view. Then I saw a grey bundle caught up in the big wheels of the semi. It looked like a sack of potatoes – rolling between the wheels.~~
It's important you know exactly what it looked like when it happened, so I've drawn a diagram for you

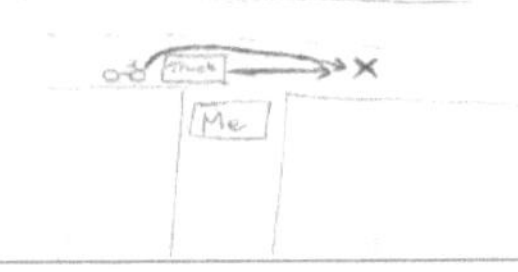

4. What does X stand for? X marks the spot.

5. The truck was a bright dirty orange, like a soiled sunrise. The cyclist was wearing a green backpack and a yellow helmet. He was young; perhaps eighteen or nineteen. He looked a little like my brother.

6. My brother lives in New York. He doesn't ride a bike, but takes the subway everywhere, or walks. Because of this, he often sees celebrities and actors on the streets of Manhattan, and asks to have his photo taken with them. I have pictures of my brother beside Robert DeNiro, Jennifer Lopez, Ricky Martin, Emilio Estevez, Mickey Rourke. But I don't have a picture of my brother beside me.

7. How is this relevant? I told you. The cyclist looked like my brother.

8. The truck passed me, blocking my view.

9. And then... X.

10. On the footpath on my side of the road were two teenage boys. They were crying ~~because they could not believe their eyes. They were crying out of shock, out of horror.~~

11. At first the driver of the semi didn't appear to realise what had happened. A hundred metres up the road he finally stopped. ~~Scattered behind his vehicle was a trail of what looked like intestines. Then, part of a body without a head. Next a patch of skin~~He got out the cab and looked down the road.
~~There was a whispering coming from inside the bubble of my car: 'No, no, no.' Then I became aware that the whispering was coming from me. What I was most aware of though, was the fraudulence of suburbia, its illusion of safety and security. I could not go to my tutorial.~~

12. Last semester in Film Studies we had looked at the Wilhelm scream. It's a sound effect of a man yelling as he falls from a cliff, recorded for the 1951 film, Distant Drums. The scream named after Private Wilhelm, the unfortunate character who died from falling. It's since been used in over two hundred movies, when characters are shot, stabbed, blown up.
The truck driver sounded a million times worse than that.

13. I couldn't go to my tutorial. I turned the car around and drove home. On the way I saw the man from the flat above ~~me~~us driving towards the intersection. ~~I wanted~~I waved at him, shouted for him to ~~tell him to go~~turn back~~, to save himself but mostly to save me. A horror witnessed by someone you know is not to be denied.~~ He called out, 'Hi!' and walked on, towards the scene of the He walked on.

14. When I got back to the flat, I didn't know what to do. I poured a glass of red wine then shoved it away. ~~I sat in the big armchair – the one that felt like it was giving me a hug but it felt like I was being smothered. I walked around the lounge room.~~ I stared out the window ~~but~~and watched for the flashing lights~~.~~. I wanted to tell someone what I'd seen but you weren't home. So I rang my mother.

15. My mother is a psychologist. I ~~needed to tell someone what I'd witnessed but my partner wasn't home. The urge was so strong I rang my parents. As~~could feel her nodding at the phone as I spoke, ~~I still hoped~~the same way that ~~I might have got it wrong. People get 'run over' or 'hit by a car'. No one told me that they get disembowelled or ripped apart. Perhaps I led too sheltered a life. I was still in my twenties and I wanted my parents to tell me that these things can't happen, that the universe forbids it. Don't happen.~~you are nodding now. All ~~they~~she could do was say ~~was~~ how awful it was. ~~My mother, a psychologist,~~She suggested that I get professional help to deal with ~~the shock of~~ what I had seen. I was indignant. Why did *I* need help? I was the lucky bystander. I was still alive. ~~It was the cyclist's parents or wife or children who would need help.~~ I told her to truck off.

~~I~~

16. Yes, I said, truck off. And when I hung up ~~and~~I could imagine her standing there, thinking, oh my poor darling, that's not even a Freudian slip. It's a Freudian *slide*.

17. I saw Barry, the drug dealer from upstairs coming up the front path.

18. His face was puffy and he was swearing to himself, which was nothing unusual, except I knew what he had seen. I had no desire to talk to him. He went upstairs and I heard muffled, urgent conversation. A few minutes later, he was heading out again with his girlfriend.

19. What kind of a name is Barry for a drug dealer, anyway?

20. Car doors slammed and an engine started. I raced outside to see them disappearing toward the intersection. ~~Anger washed over my shock.~~ I shouted after them but ~~only my ears heard~~they didn't hear me. I was still on the footpath out the front of the flats when, some minutes later, their car reappeared having done the block and was about to turn back into the street. I waited~~, ready to give Barry a piece of my mind~~ for them. But instead of turning right, he headed back to the intersection for a second look.

21. When I heard the knock I knew who it was. It wasn't enough he had had three viewings and had shown his girlfriend~~ the remains~~. Now he wanted to 'share' it with us, too. I could imagine him standing in the hallway, shuffling on the spot, his shoulders hunched. I opened the door.

22. Barry looked at me warily. He really wanted to ~~speak~~talk to ~~my partner. I told him my partner wasn't home~~you, but ~~that didn't stop him. He~~you weren't here. Yet he had something important to report and like the Ancient Mariner, he was compelled to speak. ~~And to me it was.~~

'You should've seen what happened up the road.' He waved his arm in the direction of the intersection. ~~'Gruesome –'~~

~~Normally I listened to his rambles, half annoyed, half intrigued by the unexpected things he came out with. This time, I didn't let him finish.~~

'Fucking vulture.~~'~~

~~'~~I was there,' I said. 'When he.. When it happened. I saw you take Annie for a look. Why would you *take* someone else there? To *show* them?'

~~Twenty-Five Things I am Prepared to Talk About Other Than What You Want Me to Talk About by Ryan O'Neill~~

1. It was peak hour, and the afternoon was overcast. There was a breeze coming from the southeast, and the temperature was, according to the newspaper, twenty-two degrees. The UV index was –

Yes, all that is important, but fine. I'll go on.

2. I was driving to uni with T.S. Eliot, Ted Hughes and W.H. Auden piled onto the passenger seat. There was a tutorial on Auden's *Musée des Beux Arts* at ten o'clock, and I wanted to get there early, because I hadn't read it.

3. At the end of the street was a main road with no traffic lights. Getting onto the busy thoroughfare, with cars and trucks hurtling down the hill and over the bridge across the freeway, was always difficult.

It's important you know exactly what it looked like when it happened, so I've drawn a diagram for you

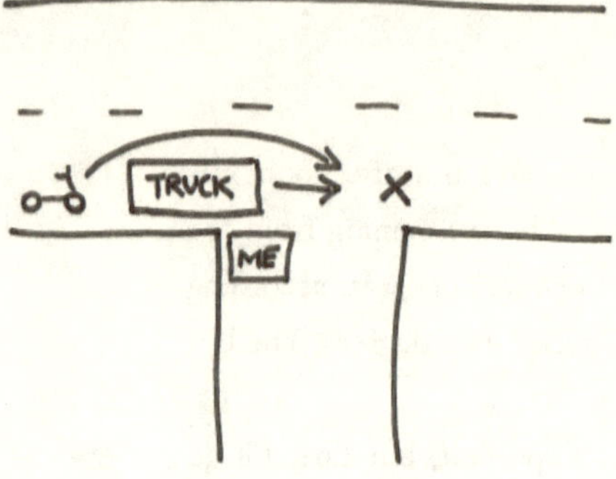

4. What does X stand for? X marks the spot.

5. The truck was a bright dirty orange, like a soiled sunrise. The cyclist was wearing a green backpack and a yellow helmet. He was young; perhaps eighteen or nineteen. He looked a little like my brother.

6. My brother lives in New York. He doesn't ride a bike, but takes the subway everywhere, or walks. Because of this, he often sees celebrities and actors on the streets of Manhattan, and asks to have his photo taken with them. I have pictures of my brother

beside Robert DeNiro, Jennifer Lopez, Ricky Martin, Emilio Estevez, Mickey Rourke. But I don't have a picture of my brother beside me.

7. How is this relevant? I told you. The cyclist looked like my brother.

8. The truck passed me, blocking my view.

9. And then... X.

10. On the footpath on my side of the road were two teenage boys. They were crying.

11. At first the driver of the semi didn't appear to realise what had happened. A hundred metres up the road he finally stopped. He got out the cab and looked down the road.

12. Last semester in Film Studies we had looked at the Wilhelm scream. It's a sound effect of a man yelling as he falls from a cliff, recorded for the 1951 film, *Distant Drums*. The scream named after Private Wilhelm, the unfortunate character who died from falling. It's since been used in over two hundred movies, when characters are shot, stabbed, blown up.

The truck driver sounded a million times worse than that.

13. I couldn't go to my tutorial. I turned the car around and drove home. On the way I saw the man from the flat above us driving towards the intersection. I waved at him, shouted for him to turn back. He called out, 'Hi!' and walked on, towards the scene of the –

He walked on.

14. When I got back to the flat, I didn't know what to do. I poured a glass of red wine then shoved it away. I stared out the window and watched for the flashing lights. I wanted to tell someone what I'd seen but you weren't home. So I rang my mother.

15. My mother is a psychologist. I could feel her nodding at the phone as I spoke, the same way that you are nodding now. All she could do was say how awful it was. She suggested that I get professional help to deal with what I had seen. I was indignant. Why did I need help? I was the lucky bystander. I was still alive. I told her to truck off.

16. Yes, I said, truck off. And when I hung up I could imagine her standing there, thinking, oh my poor darling, that's not even a Freudian slip. It's a Freudian slide.

17. I saw Barry, the drug dealer from upstairs coming up the front path.

18. His face was puffy and he was swearing to himself, which was nothing unusual, except I knew what he had seen. I had no desire to talk to him. He went upstairs and I heard muffled, urgent conversation. A few minutes later, he was heading out again with his girlfriend.

19. What kind of a name is Barry for a drug dealer, anyway?

20. Car doors slammed and an engine started. I raced outside to see them disappearing toward the intersection. I shouted after them but they didn't hear me. I was still on the footpath out the front of the flats when, some minutes later, their car reappeared having done the block and was about to turn back into the street. I waited for them. But instead of turning right, he headed back to the intersection for a second look.

21. When I heard the knock I knew who it was. It wasn't enough he had had three viewings and had shown his girlfriend. Now he wanted to 'share' it with us, too. I could imagine him standing in the hallway, shuffling on the spot, his shoulders hunched. I opened the door.

22. Barry looked at me warily. He really wanted to talk to you, but you weren't here. Yet he had something important to report and, like the Ancient Mariner, he was compelled to speak.

'You should've seen what happened up the road.' He waved his arm in the direction of the intersection.

'Fucking vulture. I was there,' I said. 'When he… When it happened. I saw you take Annie for a look. Why would you take someone else there? To show them?'

'Hey, hey,' he said. 'She rides a bike, right? I wanted her to see what can happen.'

23. He said Annie was often reckless. It wasn't enough to tell her about it. He wanted to show her something she wouldn't forget.

Well, he succeeded.

24. Later on, there was a tentative knock at the door. Barry again. He apologised for upsetting me and handed me two Valium tablets in foil. He said they would help me sleep. I told myself he meant well. I muttered 'thanks' and quickly closed the door.

25. When you came home, you saw my face and asked me what had happened. And I said I am not prepared to talk about that. And you said, what are you prepared to talk about? And so I told you.

And now you are lying beside me in bed, and I still haven't talked about what you want me to talk about. You are stroking my hair, but I feel nothing. I've taken Barry's pills, but I still can't sleep. Auden is on the bedside table, and I pick up the book and turn to the poem I was supposed to read for the tutorial.

Musée des Beux Arts

About suffering they were never wrong,
The Old Masters: how well they understood
Its human position: how it takes place
While someone else is eating or opening a window or
just walking dully along

And as I read on to the end, I feel tears filling my eyes, and I start to sob and you are holding me, and I say, 'This. I'm prepared to talk about this.'

Twenty~~-Five~~ Things I am Prepared to Talk About Other Than What You Want Me to Talk About

~~1. It was peak hour, and the afternoon was overcast. There was a breeze coming from the southeast, and the temperature was, according to the newspaper, twenty-two degrees. The UV index was- Yes, all that is important, but fine. I'll go on.~~

~~2~~1. I was driving to uni with T.S. Eliot, Ted Hughes and W.H. Auden piled onto the passenger seat. There was a tutorial on Auden's Musée des Beux Arts at ten o'clock, and I wanted to get there early, because I hadn't read it.

~~3~~2. At the end of the street was a main road with no traffic lights. Getting onto the busy thoroughfare, with cars and trucks hurtling down the hill and over the bridge across the freeway, was always difficult.
It's important you know exactly what it looked like when it happened, so I've drawn a diagram for you

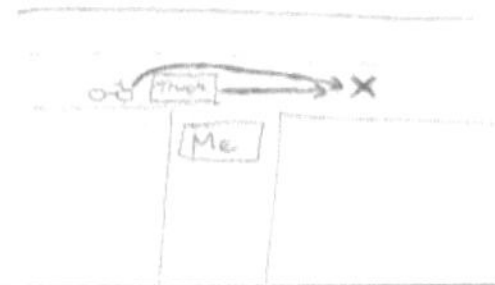

3. What does X stand for? X marks the spot.

~~5~~4. The truck was a bright dirty orange~~, like a soiled sunrise~~. The cyclist was wearing a green backpack and a yellow helmet. He was young; perhaps eighteen or nineteen. He looked a little like my brother.

~~6~~5. My brother lives in New York. He doesn't ride a bike, but takes the subway everywhere, or walks. Because of this, he often sees celebrities and actors on the streets of Manhattan, and asks to have his photo taken with them. I have pictures of my brother beside Robert DeNiro, Jennifer Lopez, Ricky Martin, Emilio Estevez, Mickey Rourke. But I don't have a picture of my brother beside me.

~~7. How is this relevant? I told you. The cyclist looked like my brother.~~

~~8~~6. The truck passed me, blocking my view.

~~9. And then~~7. Then... X.

~~10~~8. On the footpath on my side of the road were two teenage boys. They were crying.

~~11~~9. At first the driver of the semi didn't appear to realise what had happened. A hundred metres up the road he finally stopped. He got out the cab and looked down the road.

~~12~~10. Last semester in Film Studies we had looked at the Wilhelm scream. It's a sound effect of a man yelling as he falls from a cliff, recorded for the 1951 film, Distant Drums. The scream named after Private Wilhelm, the unfortunate character who died from falling. It's since been used in over two hundred movies, when characters are shot, stabbed, blown up.
The truck driver sounded a million times worse than that.

~~13~~11. I couldn't go to my tutorial. I turned the car around and drove home. On the way I saw the man from the flat above us driving towards the intersection. I waved at him, shouted for him to turn back. He called out, 'Hi!' and walked on, towards the scene of the X. ~~He walked on.~~

~~14~~
12. When I got back to the flat, I didn't know what to do. I poured a glass of red wine then ~~shoved~~pushed it away. I stared out the window and watched for the flashing lights. I wanted to tell someone what I'd seen but you weren't home. So I rang my mother.

~~15~~13. My mother is a psychologist. I could feel her nodding at the phone as I spoke, the same way that you are nodding now. All she could do was say how awful it was. She suggested that I get professional help to deal with what I had seen. I was indignant. Why did I need help? I was the lucky bystander. I was still alive. I told her to truck off.

~~16~~14. Yes, I said, truck off. And when I hung up I could imagine her standing there, thinking, oh my poor darling, that's not even a Freudian slip. It's a Freudian slide.

~~17~~15. I saw Barry, the drug dealer from upstairs coming up the front path.

~~18~~16. His face was puffy and he was swearing to himself, which was nothing unusual, except I knew what he had seen. I had no desire to talk to him. He went upstairs and I heard muffled, urgent conversation. A few minutes later, he was heading out again with his girlfriend.

~~19. What kind of a name is Barry for a drug dealer, anyway?~~

~~20. Car doors slammed and an engine started. I raced outside to see them disappearing toward the intersection. I shouted after them but they didn't hear me.~~ I was still on the footpath out the front of the flats when, some minutes later, their car reappeared having done the block and was about to turn back into the street. I waited for them. But instead of turning right, he headed back to the intersection for a second look.

~~21~~17. When I heard the knock I knew who it was. It wasn't enough he had had three viewings and had shown his girlfriend. Now he wanted to 'share' it with ~~us~~me, too. I could imagine him standing in the hallway, shuffling on the spot, his shoulders hunched. I opened the door.

~~22~~18. Barry looked at me warily. He really wanted to talk to you, but you weren't here. Yet he had something important to report and like the Ancient Mariner, he was compelled to speak.
'You should've seen what happened up the road.' He waved his arm in the direction of the intersection.
~~'Fucking vulture.~~ 'I was there,' I said. 'When he.. When it happened. I saw you take Annie for a look. Why would you *take* someone else there? To *show* them?'
'Hey, hey,' he said. 'She rides a bike, right? I wanted her to see what can happen.'

~~23. He said Annie was often reckless. It wasn't enough to tell her about it. He wanted to show her something she wouldn't forget.~~

~~Well, he succeeded.~~

~~24~~19. Later on, there was a tentative knock at the door. Barry again. He apologised for upsetting me and handed me two Valium tablets in foil. He said they would help me sleep. I told myself he meant well. I muttered 'thanks' and quickly closed the door.

~~25~~20. When you came home, you saw my face and asked me what had happened. And I said I am not prepared to talk about that. And you said, what are you prepared to talk about? And so I told you.

And now you are lying beside me in bed, and I still haven't talked about what you want me to talk about. You are stroking my hair, but I feel nothing. I've taken Barry's pills, but I still can't sleep. Auden is on the bedside table, and I pick up the book and turn to the poem I was supposed to read for the tutorial.

Musée des Beux Arts
About suffering they were never wrong,

The Old Masters: how well they understood

Its human position: how it takes place

While someone else is eating or opening a window or just walking dully along

And as I read on to the end, I feel tears filling my eyes, and I start to sob and you are holding me, and I say, 'This. I'm prepared to talk about this.'

~~Twenty Things I am Prepared to Talk About Other Than What You Want Me to Talk About by Krissy Kneen~~

1. I was driving to uni with T.S. Eliot, Ted Hughes and W.H. Auden piled onto the passenger seat. There was a tutorial on Auden's *Musée des Beux Arts* at ten o'clock, and I wanted to get there early, because I hadn't read it.

2. At the end of the street was a main road with no traffic lights. Getting onto the busy thoroughfare, with cars and trucks hurtling down the hill and over the bridge across the freeway, was always difficult.

It's important you know exactly what it looked like when it happened, so I've drawn a diagram for you

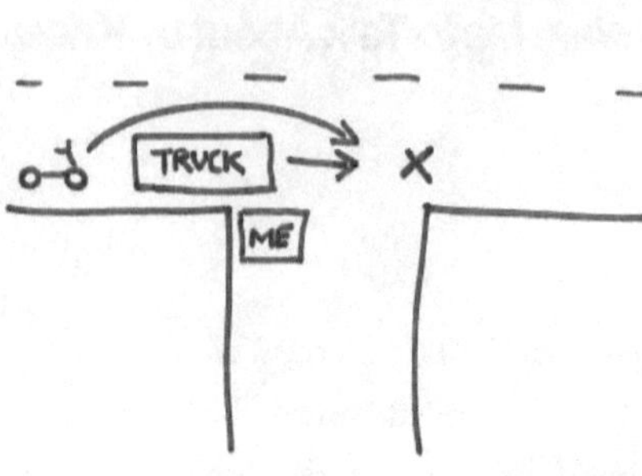

3. What does X stand for? X marks the spot.

4. The truck was a bright dirty orange. The cyclist was wearing a green backpack and a yellow helmet. He was young; perhaps eighteen or nineteen. He looked a little like my brother.

5. My brother lives in New York. He doesn't ride a bike, but takes the subway everywhere, or walks. Because of this, he often sees celebrities and actors on the streets of Manhattan, and asks to have his photo taken with them. I have pictures of my brother beside Robert DeNiro, Jennifer Lopez, Ricky Martin, Emilio Estevez, Mickey Rourke. But I don't have a picture of my brother beside me.

6. The truck passed me, blocking my view.

7. Then... X.

8. On the footpath on my side of the road were two teenage boys. They were crying.

9. At first the driver of the semi didn't appear to realise what had happened. A hundred metres up the road he finally stopped. He got out the cab and looked down the road.

10. Last semester in Film Studies we had looked at the Wilhelm scream. It's a sound effect of a man yelling as he falls from a cliff, recorded for the 1951 film, *Distant Drums*. The scream named after Private Wilhelm, the unfortunate character who died from falling. It's since been used in over two hundred movies, when characters are shot, stabbed, blown up.

The truck driver sounded a million times worse than that.

11. I couldn't go to my tutorial. I turned the car around and drove home. On the way I saw the man from the flat above us driving towards the intersection. I waved at him, shouted for

him to turn back. He called out, 'Hi!' and walked on, towards the scene of the X.

12. When I got back to the flat, I didn't know what to do. I poured a glass of red wine then pushed it away. I stared out the window and watched for the flashing lights. I wanted to tell someone what I'd seen but you weren't home. So I rang my mother.

13. My mother is a psychologist. I could feel her nodding at the phone as I spoke, the same way that you are nodding now. All she could do was say how awful it was. She suggested that I get professional help to deal with what I had seen. I was indignant. Why did I need help? I was the lucky bystander. I was still alive. I told her to truck off.

14. Yes, I said, truck off. And when I hung up I could imagine her standing there, thinking, oh my poor darling, that's not even a Freudian slip. It's a Freudian slide.

15. I saw Barry, the drug dealer from upstairs coming up the front path.

16. His face was puffy and he was swearing to himself, which was nothing unusual, except I knew what he had seen. I had no desire to talk to him. He went upstairs and I heard muffled, urgent conversation. A few minutes later, he was heading out again with his girlfriend.

I was still on the footpath out the front of the flats when, some minutes later, their car reappeared having done the block and was about to turn back into the street. I waited for them. But instead of turning right, he headed back to the intersection for a second look.

17. When I heard the knock I knew who it was. It wasn't enough he had had three viewings and had shown his girlfriend. Now he wanted to 'share' it with me, too. I could imagine him standing in the hallway, shuffling on the spot, his shoulders hunched. I opened the door.

18. Barry looked at me warily. He really wanted to talk to you, but you weren't here. Yet he had something important to report and, like the Ancient Mariner, he was compelled to speak.

'You should've seen what happened up the road.' He waved his arm in the direction of the intersection.

'I was there,' I said. 'When he… When it happened. I saw you take Annie for a look. Why would you take someone else there? To show them?'

'Hey, hey,' he said. 'She rides a bike, right? I wanted her to see what can happen.'

19. Later on, there was a tentative knock at the door. Barry again. He apologised for upsetting me and handed me two Valium tablets in foil. He said they would help me sleep. I told myself he meant well. I muttered 'thanks' and quickly closed the door.

20. When you came home, you saw my face and asked me what had happened. And I said I am not prepared to talk about that. And you said, what are you prepared to talk about? And so I told you.

And now you are lying beside me in bed, and I still haven't talked about what you want me to talk about. You are stroking my hair, but I feel nothing. I've taken Barry's pills, but I still can't sleep. Auden is on the bedside table, and I pick up the book and turn to the poem I was supposed to read for the tutorial.

Musée des Beux Arts

About suffering they were never wrong,
The Old Masters: how well they understood
Its human position: how it takes place
While someone else is eating or opening a window or
just walking dully along

And as I read on to the end, I feel tears filling my eyes, and I start to sob and you are holding me, and I say, 'This. I'm prepared to talk about this.'

Twenty Things I ~~am~~Am Prepared ~~to~~To Talk About ~~Other Than What You Want Me to Talk About~~...

~~1. I was driving to uni with T.S. Eliot, Ted Hughes and W.H. Auden piled onto the passenger seat. There was a tutorial on Auden's Musée des Beux Arts at ten o'clock, and I wanted to get there early, because I hadn't read it.~~

~~2. At the end of the street was a main road with no traffic lights. Getting onto the busy thoroughfare, with cars and trucks hurtling down the hill and over the bridge across the freeway, was always difficult.~~
~~It's important you know exactly what it looked like when it happened, so I've drawn a diagram for you~~

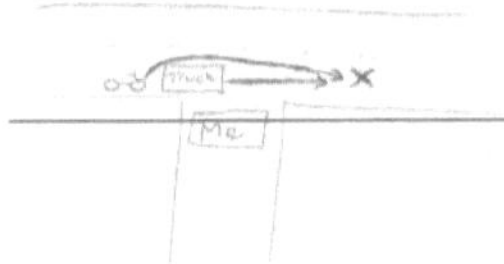

~~3. What does X stand for? X marks the spot.~~

~~4. The truck was a bright dirty orange. The cyclist was wearing a green backpack and a yellow helmet. He was young; perhaps eighteen or nineteen. He looked a little like my brother.~~

~~5. My brother lives in New York. He doesn't ride a bike, but takes the subway everywhere, or walks. Because of this, he often sees celebrities and actors on the streets of Manhattan, and asks to have his photo taken with them. I have pictures of my brother beside Robert DeNiro, Jennifer Lopez, Ricky Martin, Emilio Estevez, Mickey Rourke. But I don't have a picture of my brother beside me.~~

~~6. The truck passed me, blocking my view.~~

~~7. Then... X.~~

~~8. On the footpath on my side of the road were two teenage boys. They were crying.~~

~~9. At first the driver of the semi didn't appear to realise what had happened. A hundred metres up the road he finally stopped. He got out the cab and looked down the road.~~

~~10. Last semester in Film Studies we had looked at the Wilhelm scream. It's a sound effect of a man yelling as he falls from a cliff, recorded for the 1951 film, Distant Drums. The scream named after Private Wilhelm, the unfortunate character who died from falling. It's since been used in over two hundred movies, when characters are shot, stabbed, blown up.~~
~~The truck driver sounded a million times worse than that.~~

~~11. I couldn't go to my tutorial. I turned the car around and drove home. On the way I saw the man from the flat above us driving towards the intersection. I waved at him, shouted for him to turn back. He called out, 'Hi!' and walked on, towards the scene of the X.~~

~~12. When I got back to the flat, I didn't know what to do. I poured a glass of red wine then pushed it away. I stared out the window and watched for the flashing lights. I wanted to tell someone what I'd seen but you weren't home. So I rang my mother.~~

~~13. My mother is a psychologist. I could feel her nodding at the phone as I spoke, the same way that you are nodding now. All she could do was say how awful it was. She suggested that I get professional help to deal with what I had seen. I was indignant. Why did I need help? I was the lucky bystander. I was still alive. I told her to truck off.~~

~~14. Yes, I said, truck off. And when I hung up I could imagine her standing there, thinking, oh my poor darling, that's not even a Freudian slip. It's a Freudian slide.~~

~~15. I saw Barry, the drug dealer from upstairs coming up the front path.~~

~~16. His face was puffy and he was swearing to himself, which was nothing unusual, except I knew what he had seen. I had no desire to talk to him. He went upstairs and I heard muffled, urgent conversation. A few minutes later, he was heading out again with his girlfriend.~~
~~I was still on the footpath out the front of the flats when, some minutes later,~~

~~their car reappeared having done the block and was about to turn back into the street. I waited for them. But instead of turning right, he headed back to the intersection for a second look.~~

~~17. When I heard the knock I knew who it was. It wasn't enough he had had three viewings and had shown his girlfriend. Now he wanted to 'share' it with me, too. I could imagine him standing in the hallway, shuffling on the spot, his shoulders hunched. I opened the door.~~

~~18. Barry looked at me warily. He really wanted to talk to you, but you weren't here. Yet he had something important to report and like the Ancient Mariner, he was compelled to speak.~~
~~'You should've seen what happened up the road.' He waved his arm in the direction of the intersection.~~
~~'I was there,' I said. 'When he... When it happened. I saw you take Annie for a look. Why would you take someone else there? To show them?'~~
~~'Hey, hey,' he said. 'She rides a bike, right? I wanted her to see what can happen.'~~

~~19. Later on, there was a tentative knock at the door. Barry again. He apologised for upsetting me and handed me two Valium tablets in foil. He said they would help me sleep. I told myself he meant well. I muttered 'thanks' and quickly closed the door.~~

~~20. When you came home, you saw my face and asked me what had happened. And I said I am not prepared to talk about that. And you said, what are you prepared to talk about? And so I told you.~~
~~And now you are lying beside me in bed, and I still haven't talked about what you want me to talk about. You are stroking my hair, but I feel nothing. I've taken Barry's pills, but I still can't sleep. Auden is on the bedside table, and I pick up the book and turn to the poem I was supposed to read for the tutorial.~~

~~Musée des Beux Arts~~
About suffering they were never wrong,

The Old Masters: how well they understood

Its human position~~:~~, how it takes place

While someone ~~else is eating or opening a window~~is waiting bored at an intersection or just ~~walking~~driving dully along,

~~And as I read on to the end, I feel tears filling my eyes, and I start to sob and you are holding me, and I say, 'This. I'm prepared to talk about this.'~~How, when some are reverently, passionately waiting
For miraculous comprehension, there must always be
Some other lowlife who seemed to feel nothing, who went
Galvanized, greedy, back for a second look:
While a young boy on a bike, left
As just a figure marked with an x in a diagram now, was the one
To let the dreadful martyrdom run its course.
Anyhow we turn the car around, cast about bereft
For connections back home, find distractions in celebrity names,
Ring our mother, accept we are bystanders; take a couple of Valiums.

In Walsh's *Distant Drums*, for instance, how a character, at his death
Screams as he falls, creating a classic movie meme –
The sound effect of that last anguished breath
An in-joke now for Spielberg, Lucas, Tarantino; no matter how extreme
The CGI, nothing about this is manufactured. You may
Have heard the raw forsaken cry, and looked away
From the driver's own anguish, the fleeting flash of green
Backpack, two teenage boys weeping at what they had seen:
Something amazing, a boy falling out of the sky,
The intersection one giant X, traffic eventually rolling calmly on.

Nothing helps us sleep now. Masterful Auden
Waits for us – patient, sorrowful – on the bedside table.

~~Twenty Things I am Prepared To Talk About… by Cate Kennedy~~

About suffering they were never wrong,
The Old Masters: how well they understood
Its human position; how it takes place
While someone is waiting bored at an intersection or just driving dully along;
How, when some are reverently, passionately waiting
For miraculous comprehension, there must always be
Some other lowlife who seemed to feel nothing, who went
Galvanized, greedy, back for a second look:
While a young boy on a bike, left
As just a figure marked with an x in a diagram now, was the one
To let the dreadful martyrdom run its course.
Anyhow we turn the car around, cast about bereft
For connections back home, find distractions in celebrity names,
Ring our mother, accept we are bystanders; take a couple of Valiums.

In Walsh's *Distant Drums*, for instance, how a character, at his death
Screams as he falls, creating a classic movie meme –

The sound effect of that last anguished breath
An in-joke now for Spielberg, Lucas, Tarantino; no matter
how extreme
The CGI, nothing about this is manufactured. You may
Have heard the raw forsaken cry, and looked away
From the driver's own anguish, the fleeting flash of green
Backpack, two teenage boys weeping at what they had seen:
Something amazing, a boy falling out of the sky,
The intersection one giant X, traffic eventually rolling calmly
on.

Nothing helps us sleep now. Masterful Auden
Waits for us – patient, sorrowful – on the bedside table.

~~My Father as a Short Story by Ryan O'Neill~~

Beginning

On the third floor of the tenement building in the east end of Glasgow, where my father was born on 20 July 1935... Or at St Bridget's chapel in Edinburgh where my father and mother were married on 3 August 1971... Or on my parents' bedroom floor, where my father lay for three hours after having a stroke on the morning of 5 February 1989... Or by my mother's hospital bed in Glasgow Royal Infirmary when she died on 29 November 2011... Or 18 March 2012, the last time I spoke to my father.

Genre

Alternative History: My father is not invited to the wedding in 1969 where he meets my mother, and I am never born.

Fantasy: Typing the words, 'My father often told me that he loved me' would make them true.

Mystery: It turns out I killed my father by fracturing his skull with an encyclopaedia.

Romance: No. I can't imagine my father in a romance.

Humorous: On seeing a notice on the wall of my grandmother's bathroom, 'What would Jesus do?' my father added, 'Wipe his arse, I would hope.'

Conflict

My father versus me.

or

My father versus my mother.

or

My father versus our neighbour's cat.

or

My father versus the postman.

or

My father versus Glasgow City Council.

or

My father versus the British Royal Family.

or

My father versus Christianity.

or

My father versus my father.

Characterisation

Explicit: When my father was eight years old, he was badly beaten by an older boy at school. When my grandfather discovered this, he forced my father to fight the boy once a week until my father won. This took four years.

Implicit: My father did his National Service in Egypt. Though he hated the army, he was soon promoted to corporal, and made an officer's servant, or 'batman'. One of his duties was to serve his officer tea in bed in the morning. Before adding the hot water, my father would spit in the mug.

Complication

Comparing the dates on my birth certificate, and my parents' wedding certificate, I realised the two dates were only six months apart.

'Well, why did you think we got married?' my father said.

Dialogue

My father speaks in a Glaswegian dialect that doesn't translate well to the page. The ellipses and repetition caused by his stroke, and his use of the word 'fuck' as noun, verb, adjective, preposition, adverb, pronoun and conjunction also causes problems. Yet translating his words into Standard English makes them lose much of their character, as can be seen in the example below, taken from our last conversation two years ago.

How my father talks (Original)	How my father talks (Translated)
Och, Ah doan't no son. Ma fuckin' leegs are fucked, ye knaw? Ah'm gettin' auld, it's awfy fuckin' rottun son, so it is. Lissen noo, hoo's the weans? Hoo's… Whit's 'er name… Hoo's yer wife? Tell um Ah wiz askin' fur um, wull ye? Haud oan a fuckin' minute. Ah huv tae sit doon. Aw, Christ, Ah miss yer maw, so Ah fuckin' dae. Ah miss... Fur fuck's sake! Hauld on! My fuckin' brain's fuckin' fucked, thit's whit's wrang. Ah, Christ! Don't google ut me like Ah'm fuckin' daft. Whit the fuck'd ye knaw anyway? She hudnae seen ye for three years, ye reed-heeded bastard. Away tae fuck!	Oh, I don't know, son. My legs are very sore. I'm getting old. It's not nice. How are your children? And your wife? Please give them my regards. Now wait a moment. I need to sit down. Oh God, I miss your mother. Oh, for goodness sake! Wait a moment. My mind is playing tricks on me. That's the problem. Oh God. Don't stare at me as if I am stupid. I'm not. What would you know about loss anyway? You hadn't seen your mother for three years. You're no son of mine. Go away.

Symbolism

After school finished I would walk to the warehouse where my father worked for a protective footwear and clothing company. I was allowed to play there, if I kept out of the way. I would pull blue overalls over my school uniform, and put on a gas mask, earplugs, helmet, and huge steel-capped boots. Then I would walk slowly round the warehouse, listening to the sound of my own breathing.

Foreshadowing

Every year I can recall my father counting how many years he had left before retiring at sixty-five, when he promised himself he would spend all his time reading.

Dramatic Irony

At fifty-four he had a stroke, and was never able to read another book, including my own, published twelve years later.

Character Arc

My father's qualities

Beginning of story	**End of Story**
Undemonstrative	Undemonstrative
Irritable	Irritable
Vulgar	Vulgar
Generous	Generous
Intolerant	Intolerant

Plot

A writer eventually realises the futility of attempting to translate his father into a form the writer can understand.

Round Characters

My father.

Flat Characters

My mother.

A doctor.

Several nurses.

Cousins, aunts and uncles.

Me.

Epiphany

One afternoon last year, I had to sit in a crowded waiting room for an hour and a half before I could see a doctor. I soon finished the novel I was reading, and all the magazines were already taken, so for something to read I picked a pamphlet at random from a plastic rack on the wall. When I finished it, I realised that my father had been depressed for most of his adult life. And so, it turned out, had I.

Ending

A Twist Ending: My father died when I was two years old. I don't remember anything about him.

A Closed Ending: After finishing this story, I never write or think about my father again.

An Open Ending: At nine o'clock at night here, it is eight o'clock in the morning in Scotland. If I call, my father will probably be in the kitchen when he hears the phone ringing. It might take a moment or two, as he is getting deaf. The phone is in the hallway, and he is always out of breath by the time he reaches it.

'Hello?' he'll say. 'Hello?'

'It's me.' I'll say. 'Your son.'

My Father as a Short Story

~~**Beginning**~~

~~On the third floor of the tenement building in the east end of Glasgow, where my father was born on 20 July 1935... Or at St Bridget's chapel in Edinburgh where my father and mother were married on 3 August 1971... Or on my parents' bedroom floor, where my father lay for three hours after having a stroke on the morning of 5 February 1989... Or by my mother's hospital bed in Glasgow Royal Infirmary when she died on 29 November 2011... Or March 18 2012, the last time I spoke to my father.~~
~~**Genre**~~

~~Alternative History: My father is not invited to the wedding in 1969 where he meets my mother, and I am never born.~~
~~Fantasy: Typing the words, 'My father often told me that he loved me' would make them true.~~
~~Mystery: It turns out I killed my father by fracturing his skull with an encyclopaedia.~~
~~Romance: No. I can't imagine my father in a romance.~~
~~Humorous: On seeing a notice on the wall of my grandmother's bathroom, 'What would Jesus do?' my father added, 'Wipe his arse, I would hope.'~~
~~**Conflict**~~

~~My father versus me~~
~~or~~
~~My father versus my mother~~
~~or~~
~~My father versus our neighbour's cat.~~
~~or~~
~~My father versus the postman.~~
~~or~~
~~My father versus Glasgow city council.~~
~~or~~
~~My father versus the British Royal Family.~~
~~or~~
~~My father versus Christianity.~~
~~or~~
~~My father versus my father.~~
~~**Characterisation**~~

~~*Explicit*: When my father was eight years old, he was badly beaten by an older boy at school. When my grandfather discovered this, he forced my father to fight the boy once a week until my father won.~~ The writer's father was gone and nothing could change that. But writing could perform miracles that life didn't permit. It could resurrect people from the dead and that's what he wanted to do, to bring his father to life on the page if not in the world.
He had thought that death would clarify things, that his father would develop sharp outlines like a character in a book, that his life would take on a satisfying shape, that he would finally make sense to him in a way that he hadn't in life. But his father had always been an ornery character. When he did his National Service in Egypt, he was~~This took four years.~~

~~*Implicit*: My father did his National Service in Egypt. Though he hated the army, he was soon~~ promoted to corporal, and made an officer's servant, or 'batman'. One of his duties was to serve his officer tea in bed in the morning. Before adding the hot water, ~~my father would spit in the mug.~~ his father would spit in the mug. The writer couldn't shake the feeling that his father would regard his story with the same disdain. That he would sabotage it from the grave. He always had to have the last word.
~~**Complication**~~

How to begin? The obvious place to start was his father's birth on the third floor of the tenement building in the east end of Glasgow, on 20 July 1935... Or maybe St Bridget's chapel in Edinburgh where his father and mother were married on 3 August 1971... More dramatic would be his parents' bedroom floor, where his father lay for three hours after having a stroke on the morning of 5 February 1989... Or his mother's hospital bed in Glasgow Royal Infirmary when she died on 29 November 2011... If it was going to be about their relationship, perhaps the place to start was the end, the last time he spoke to his father on March 18 2012. The problem was that these openings were so open-ended, he didn't know where to go from there. What he was left with were resolutely stubborn facts that refused to be massaged into something larger and more meaningful. It occurred to him that perhaps he was being too literal-minded, that he was allowing himself to be straight-jacketed by the conventions of realism. Perhaps he needed to loosen up, to embrace other genres that might release his inner father, might set him free. He contemplated the possibilities. An alternative history, a counter-factual could be interesting. What if his father had not been invited to the wedding in 1969 where he met his mother, and the writer had never born? But that was an obvious non-starter. No writer, no story.

He flirted with the idea of a mystery in which he kills his father by fracturing his skull with an encyclopaedia. But that might look like he'd misunderstood Freud. His father might be a mystery to him but killing him wouldn't solve the mystery.

He flirted even more briefly with the idea of a romance but couldn't imagine his father in a romance. Comparing the dates on ~~my~~his birth certificate, and ~~my~~his parents' wedding certificate, ~~I~~the writer realised the two dates were only six months apart.

'Well, why did you think we got married?' ~~my~~his father said.
~~Dialogue~~

~~My father speaks in a Glaswegian dialect that doesn't~~For a while, writing a comic portrait seemed the obvious option. He thought about all the stories he could tell. On seeing a notice on the wall of his grandmother's bathroom 'What would Jesus do?', his father added, 'Wipe his arse, I would hope.' And then there was the way his father spoke, which some people seemed to find funny. Och, Ah doan't no son. Ma fuckin' leegs are fucked, ye knaw? Ah'm gettin' auld, it's awfy fuckin' rottun son, so it is. Lissen noo, hoo's the weans? Hoo's.. Whit's 'er name... Hoo's yer wife? Tell um Ah wiz askin' fur um, wull ye? Haud oan a fuckin' minute. Ah huv tae sit doon. (Oh, I don't know, son. My legs are very sore. I'm getting old. It's not nice. How are your children? And your wife? Please give them my regards. Now wait a moment. I need to sit down.) Aw, Christ. Ah miss yer maw, so Ah fuckin' dae. Ah miss... Fur fuck's sake! Hauld on! My fuckin' brain's fuckin' fucked, thit's whit's wrang. Ah, Christ! Don't google ut me like Ah'm fuckin' daft. Whit the fuck'd ye knaw anyway? She hudnae seen ye for three years, ye reed-heeded bastard. Away tae fuck! (Oh God, I miss your mother. Oh, for goodness sake! Wait a moment. My mind is playing tricks on me. That's the problem. Oh God. Don't stare at me as if I am stupid. I'm not. What would you know about loss anyway? You hadn't seen your mother for three years. You're no son of mine. Go away.)

But it worried him that his father's Glaswegian dialect didn't translate well to the page. The ellipses and repetition caused by his stroke, and his use of the word 'fuck' as noun, verb, adjective, preposition, adverb, pronoun and conjunction also causes problems. Yet translating his words into Standard English ~~makes~~made them lose much of their character~~.~~. Tragi-comic as ~~can be seen in the example below, taken from our~~it might sound, this had been his last conversation ~~two years ago~~with his father, a fact which somewhat blunted its comic edge.

In desperation, he decided to cut loose and try fantasy. All the wrongs of their relationship could be righted. If only typing the words, 'My father often told me that he loved me' would make them true. But it didn't. And in the end, he had to write what was true. Why couldn't he just tell it how it was? It wasn't as though his father's life lacked drama or conflict. His father was always at logger-heads with someone. His wife, his son, his neighbour's cat, the postman, the Glasgow city council, the British Royal Family, Christianity, himself. None of this was surprising when you knew that when he was eight years old he was badly beaten by an older boy at school. When the writer's grandfather discovered this, he forced his father to fight the boy once a week until his father won. This took four years.

~~My Father as a Short Story by Fiona Capp~~

The writer's father was gone and nothing could change that. But writing could perform miracles that life didn't permit. It could resurrect people from the dead and that's what he wanted to do, to bring his father to life on the page if not in the world.

He had thought that death would clarify things, that his father would develop sharp outlines like a character in a book, that his life would take on a satisfying shape, that he would finally make sense to him in a way that he hadn't in life. But his father had always been an ornery character. When he did his National Service in Egypt, he was promoted to corporal, and made an officer's servant, or 'batman'. One of his duties was to serve his officer tea in bed in the morning. Before adding the hot water, his father would spit in the mug. The writer couldn't shake the feeling that his father would regard his story with the same disdain. That he would sabotage it from the grave. He always had to have the last word.

How to begin? The obvious place to start was his father's birth on the third floor of the tenement building in the east end of Glasgow, on 20 July 1935... Or maybe St Bridget's chapel in Edinburgh where his father and mother were married on 3 August 1971... More dramatic would be his parents' bedroom floor, where his father lay for three hours after having a stroke on the morning of 5 February 1989... Or his mother's hospital bed in Glasgow Royal Infirmary when she died on 29 November 2011... If it was going to be about their relationship, perhaps the place to start was the end, the last time he spoke to his father on 18 March 2012.

The problem was that these openings were so open-ended, he didn't know where to go from there. What he was left with were resolutely stubborn facts that refused to be massaged into something larger and more meaningful. It occurred to him that perhaps he was being too literal-minded, that he was allowing himself to be straight-jacketed by the conventions of realism. Perhaps he needed to loosen up, to embrace other genres that might release his inner father, might set him free. He contemplated the possibilities. An alternative history, a counter-factual could be interesting.

What if his father had not been invited to the wedding in 1969 where he met his mother, and the writer had never born? But that was an obvious non-starter. No writer, no story.

He flirted with the idea of a mystery in which he kills his father by fracturing his skull with an encyclopaedia. But that might look like he'd misunderstood Freud. His father might be a mystery to him but killing him wouldn't solve the mystery.

He flirted even more briefly with the idea of a romance but couldn't imagine his father in a romance. Comparing the dates on his birth certificate, and his parents' wedding certificate, the writer realised the two dates were only six months apart. 'Well, why did you think we got married?' his father said.

For a while, writing a comic portrait seemed the obvious option. He thought about all the stories he could tell. On seeing a notice on the wall of his grandmother's bathroom 'What would Jesus do?', his father added, 'Wipe his arse, I would hope.' And then there was the way his father spoke, which some people seemed to find funny. Och, Ah doan't no son. Ma fuckin' leegs are fucked, ye knaw? Ah'm gettin' auld, it's awfy fuckin' rottun son, so it is. Lissen noo, hoo's the weans? Hoo's…

Whit's 'er name… Hoo's yer wife? Tell um Ah wiz askin' fur um, wull ye? Haud oan a fuckin' minute. Ah huv tae sit doon. (Oh, I don't know, son. My legs are very sore. I'm getting old. It's not nice. How are your children? And your wife? Please give them my regards. Now wait a moment. I need to sit down.) Aw, Christ, Ah miss yer maw, so Ah fuckin' dae. Ah miss... Fur fuck's sake! Hauld on! My fuckin' brain's fuckin' fucked, thit's whit's wrang. Ah, Christ! Don't google ut me like Ah'm fuckin' daft. Whit the fuck'd ye knaw anyway? She hudnae seen ye for three years, ye reed-heeded bastard. Away tae fuck! (Oh God, I miss your mother. Oh, for goodness sake! Wait a moment. My mind is playing tricks on me. That's the problem. Oh God. Don't stare at me as if I am stupid. I'm not. What would you know about loss anyway? You hadn't seen your mother for three years. You're no son of mine. Go away.)

But it worried him that his father's Glaswegian dialect didn't translate well to the page. The ellipses and repetition caused by his stroke, and his use of the word 'fuck' as noun, verb, adjective, preposition, adverb, pronoun and conjunction also causes problems. Yet translating his words into Standard English made them lose much of their character. Tragicomic as it might sound, this had been his last conversation with his father, a fact which somewhat blunted its comic edge.

In desperation, he decided to cut loose and try fantasy. All the wrongs of their relationship could be righted. If only typing the words, 'My father often told me that he loved me' would make them true. But it didn't. And in the end, he had to write what was true. Why couldn't he just tell it how it was? It wasn't as though his father's life lacked drama or conflict. His father was always at logger-heads with someone. His wife, his son, his neighbour's cat, the postman, the Glasgow City Council, the British Royal Family, Christianity, himself. None of this was surprising when you knew that when he was eight years old he was badly beaten by an older boy at school. When the writer's grandfather discovered this, he forced his father to fight the boy once a week until his father won. This took four years.

Every year of his working life, his father counted how many years he had left before retiring at sixty-five, when he promised himself he would spend all his time reading. At fifty-four he had a stroke, and was never able to read another book, including the writer's own, published twelve years later. If his father had been transformed by this blow, if he had mellowed or become angrier or more reflective, it would have give the writer a chance to capture the poignancy of his father's plight. But his father remained unrepentantly unchanged. The same undemonstrative, irritable, vulgar, generous and intolerant man he'd always been.

One afternoon last year, the writer had an epiphany while sitting in a crowded waiting room for an hour and a half before he could see a doctor. He soon finished the novel he was reading, and all the magazines were already taken, so for something to read he picked a pamphlet at random from a plastic rack on the wall. When he finished it, he realised that his father had been depressed for most of his adult life. And so, it turned out, had he.

That night he went to bed early and was in that state between waking and dreaming when your mind does strange things. He was thinking about how it would be breakfast time in Scotland, the hour that his father used to call, on the rare occasions that he did. And then the writer's phone started ringing at the other end of his house. As he scrambled out of bed, he could see his father standing in the hallway of his house in Scotland, the phone pressed to his ear. The phone switched on to the answering machine just before the writer could reach it.

'Hello?' he heard his father say. 'Hello?'

My Father as a Short Story

~~The writer's father was gone and nothing could change that. But writing could perform miracles that life didn't permit. It could resurrect people from the dead and that's what he wanted to do, to bring his father to life on the page if not in the world.~~
~~He had thought that death would clarify things, that his father would develop sharp outlines like a character in a book, that his life would take on a satisfying shape, that he would finally make sense to him in a way that he hadn't in life. But his father had always been an ornery character. When he did his National Service in Egypt, he was promoted to corporal, and made an officer's servant, or 'batman'. One~~The father spat on the writer's story.
When the writer's father did his National Service in Egypt, one of his duties was to serve his officer tea in bed in the morning. Before adding the hot water, his father would spit in the mug. ~~The writer couldn't shake the feeling that his father would regard his story with the same disdain. That he would sabotage it from the grave. He always had to have the last word.~~
~~How to begin? The obvious place to start was his father's birth~~Later, the writer was looking through the manuscript about his father. He touched the page, found the paper slick with the slime of spit. He took it as a criticism, reading over the words that were worthy of derision. He picked up the wad of paper and placed it warily in the recycling bin.
He began again. This time the story started with the writer's father being born on the third floor of the tenement building in the east end of Glasgow, on 20 July 1935~~... Or maybe~~. The writer came back to the manuscript and put his hand on the baby's chest and found there was no breath in him. A father still-born. The death of a writer.
St Bridget's chapel in Edinburgh where his father and mother were married on 3 August 1971~~... More dramatic would be his parents' bedroom floor, where his father lay for~~. Words raining down on the blank pages with the dry rustle of thrown rice. Over the next three ~~hours after having a stroke on the morning of 5 February 1989... Or his mother's hospital bed in Glasgow Royal Infirmary when she died on 29 November 2011... If it was going to be about their relationship, perhaps the place to start was the end, the last time he spoke to his father on March 18 2012~~ days the rice swelled. A blue mould set in, changing the scent of the words. The writer could not read his own work without feeling slightly nauseous.
~~The problem was that these openings were so open-ended, he didn't know where to go from there. What he was left with were resolutely stubborn facts that refused to be massaged into something larger and more meaningful. It occurred to him that perhaps he was being too literal-minded, that he was allowing himself to be straight-jacketed by the conventions of realism. Perhaps he needed to loosen up, to embrace other genres that might release his inner father, might set him free. He contemplated the possibilities. An alternative history, a counter-factual could be interesting. What if his father had not been invited to the wedding in 1969 where he met his mother, and the writer had never born? But that was an obvious non-starter. No writer, no story. He flirted with the idea of a mystery in which he~~Fresh clean pages and the writer's father collapsing on them, folded to the floor and resting there, damaged, the blood leaking out into his brain for three treacherous hours. 5 February 1989. After the stroke the writer's father lost the power of language, he stared out from the dumb pages, frustrated and in pain. When the writer tried to move him from one page to the other he discovered that the man could barely limp through the narrative.
And so, beginning at the end, the writer chose a circling narrative. The last conversation between the writer and his father. 18 March 2012. The writer recorded each sentence, word by word and yet when he read back over the work he discovered there was no content, no meaning. The words were barely recognisable, providing no meaning and no context.
More paper for the recycling bin.
He flirted with the idea of a mystery in which the writer kills his father by fracturing his skull with an encyclopaedia. ~~But that might look like he'd misunderstood~~ Freud~~. His~~ nodded his sage head. Free of the spectre of his father~~ might be a mystery to him but killing him wouldn't solve the mystery.~~

~~He flirted even more briefly with the idea of a romance but couldn't imagine his father in a romance. Comparing the dates on his birth certificate, and his parents' wedding certificate~~, the writer ~~realised the two dates were only six months apart. 'Well, why did you think we got married?' his father said.~~

~~For a while, writing a comic portrait seemed the obvious option. He thought about all the stories he could tell. On seeing a notice on the wall of his grandmother's bathroom 'What would Jesus do?', his father added, 'Wipe his arse, I would hope.' And then there~~ was ~~the way his father spoke, which some people seemed~~now free to make passionate love to ~~find funny. Och, Ah doan't no son. Ma fuckin' leegs are fucked, ye knaw? Ah'm gettin' auld, it's awfy fuckin' rottun son, so it is. Lissen noo, hoo's the weans? Hoo's... Whit's 'er name... Hoo's yer wife? Tell um Ah wiz askin' fur um, wull ye? Haud oan a fuckin' minute. Ah huv tae sit doon. (Oh, I don't know, son. My legs are very sore. I'm getting old. It's not nice. How are your children? And your wife? Please give them my regards. Now wait a moment. I need to sit down.) Aw, Christ, Ah miss yer maw, so Ah fuckin' dae. Ah miss... Fur fuck's sake! Hauld on! My fuckin' brain's fuckin' fucked, thit's whit's wrang. Ah, Christ! Don't google ut me like Ah'm fuckin' daft. Whit the fuck'd ye knaw anyway? She hudnae seen ye for three years, ye reed-heeded bastard. Away tae fuck! (Oh God, I miss your~~ his mother. ~~Oh~~The writer reached for ~~goodness sake! Wait a moment. My mind is playing tricks on me. That's the problem. Oh God. Don't stare at me as if I am stupid. I'm not. What would you know about loss anyway? You hadn't seen your mother for three years. You're no son of mine. Go away.)~~

~~But it worried him that his father's Glaswegian dialect didn't translate well to the page. The ellipses and repetition caused by his stroke, and his use of the word 'fuck' as noun, verb, adjective, preposition, adverb, pronoun and conjunction also causes problems. Yet translating his words into Standard English made them lose much of their character. Tragi-comic as it might sound, this had been his last conversation with his father, a fact which somewhat blunted its comic edge.~~ her brassiere. The writer stopped, tore up the offending page.

In desperation, he decided to ~~cut loose~~shake off the shackles of the real world and try fantasy. All the wrongs of their relationship could be righted. ~~If only typing~~Typing the words, 'My father often told me that he loved me' would make them true. ~~But it didn't. And in the end, he had to write what was true. Why couldn't he just tell it how it was? It wasn't as though his father's~~ He typed the words and his father spoke them, but the corner of his mouth turned upward in a sneer and the words were damaged by his inflection.

His father needed an easier life ~~lacked drama or conflict. His father was always at logger-heads with someone. His wife, his son, his neighbour's cat, the postman, the Glasgow city council, the British Royal Family, Christianity, himself. None of this was surprising when you knew that when he was eight years old he was badly beaten by an older~~. He needed joy. The writer rewrote his father's childhood. Removing the boy ~~at~~ who used to beat him up each afternoon after school. ~~When the writer's grandfather discovered this, he forced his father to fight the boy once a week until his father won. This took four years~~He invented a long and lovely romance for his parents, a wedding dress for his mother that was tight about her waist because in this version of her life she was not already pregnant. He cleared the blockage in his father's brain and blessed his future with language. In this new, forgiving narrative his father published books, became a celebrated author. The writer stood in line at his father's book launch. He pressed the book open to the title page. *To my son,* wrote his father, pausing. The writer was in charge of the story. The writer held his father's pen. *With love.* The writer made the marks on the page, but when the father pushed the book across the signing table there was an ironic underline under the word *love*. There were little hearts and crosses. His father grinned like a manic cherub. The writer glanced down to see the edges of the heart dissolving. His father had, yet again, spat on the page.

~~My Father as a Short Story by Krissy Kneen~~

The father spat on the writer's story.

When the writer's father did his National Service in Egypt, one of his duties was to serve his officer tea in bed in the morning. Before adding the hot water, his father would spit in the mug.

Later, the writer was looking through the manuscript about his father. He touched the page, found the paper slick with the slime of spit. He took it as a criticism, reading over the words that were worthy of derision. He picked up the wad of paper and placed it warily in the recycling bin.

He began again. This time the story started with the writer's father being born on the third floor of the tenement building in the east end of Glasgow, on 20 July 1935. The writer came back to the manuscript and put his hand on the baby's chest and found there was no breath in him. A father still-born. The death of a writer.

St Bridget's chapel in Edinburgh where his father and mother were married on 3 August

1971. Words raining down on the blank pages with the dry rustle of thrown rice. Over the next three days the rice swelled. A blue mould set in, changing the scent of the words. The writer could not read his own work without feeling slightly nauseous.

Fresh clean pages and the writer's father collapsing on them, folded to the floor and resting there, damaged, the blood leaking out into his brain for three treacherous hours. 5 February 1989. After the stroke the writer's father lost the power of language, he stared out from the dumb pages, frustrated and in pain. When the writer tried to move him from one page to the other he discovered that the man could barely limp through the narrative.

And so, beginning at the end, the writer chose a circling narrative. The last conversation between the writer and his father. 18 March 2012. The writer recorded each sentence, word by word and yet when he read back over the work he discovered there was no content, no meaning. The words were barely recognisable, providing no meaning and no context.

More paper for the recycling bin.

He flirted with the idea of a mystery in which the writer kills his father by fracturing his skull with an encyclopaedia. Freud nodded his sage head. Free of the spectre of his father, the writer was now free to make passionate love to his mother. The writer reached for her brassiere. The writer stopped, tore up the offending page.

In desperation, he decided to shake off the shackles of the real world and try fantasy. All the wrongs of their relationship could be righted. Typing the words, 'My father often told me that he loved me' would make them true. He typed the words and his father spoke them, but the corner of his mouth turned upward in a sneer and the words were damaged by his inflection.

His father needed an easier life. He needed joy. The writer rewrote his father's childhood. Removing the boy who used to beat him up each afternoon after school. He invented a long and lovely romance for his parents, a wedding dress for his mother that was tight about her waist because in this version of her life she was not already pregnant. He cleared the blockage in his father's brain and blessed his future with language. In this new, forgiving narrative his father published books, became a celebrated author. The writer stood in line at his father's book launch. He pressed the book open to the title page. To my son, wrote his father, pausing. The writer was in charge of the story. The writer held his father's pen. With love. The writer made the marks on the page, but when the father pushed the book across the signing table there was an ironic underline under the word love. There were little hearts and crosses. His father grinned like a manic cherub. The writer glanced down to see the edges of the heart dissolving. His father had, yet again, spat on the page.

One afternoon last year, the writer had an epiphany while sitting in a crowded waiting room for an hour and a half before he could see a doctor. He soon finished the novel he was reading, and all the magazines were already taken, so for something to read he picked a pamphlet at random from a plastic rack on the wall. When he finished it, he realised that his father had been depressed for most of his adult life. And so, it turned out, had he.

That night he went to bed early and was in that state between waking and dreaming when your mind does strange things. He was thinking about how it would be breakfast time in Scotland, the hour that his father used to call, on the rare occasions that he did. And then the writer's phone started ringing at the other end of his house.

He scrambled out of bed. He stopped. He could see his father standing in the hallway of his house in Scotland, the phone pressed to his ear.

The phone switched on to the answering machine just before the writer could reach it.

'Hello?' he heard his father say. 'Hello?'

My Father as a Short Story

~~The father spat on the writer's story.~~
~~When the writer's father did his National Service in Egypt, one of his duties was to serve his officer tea in bed in the morning. Before adding the hot water, his father would spit in the mug.~~
~~Later, the writer was looking through the manuscript about his father. He touched the page, found the paper slick with the slime of spit. He took it as a criticism, reading over the words that were worthy of derision. He picked up the wad of paper and placed it warily in the recycling bin.~~

~~He began again. This time the story~~I started ~~with the writer's~~logically, or tried to. My father~~ being~~, born on the third floor of the tenement building in the east end of Glasgow, on 20 July 1935. ~~The writer came back to the manuscript and~~I wrote these words then felt the story fall fatally silent. I put ~~his~~my hand on the baby's chest and found there was no breath in him. A father still-born. ~~The death of a writer.~~

I began again. St Bridget's chapel in Edinburgh, where ~~his~~my father and mother were married on 3 August 1971. Words raining down on the blank pages with the dry rustle of thrown rice. Over the next three days the rice swelled. A blue mould set in, changing the scent of the words. ~~The writer~~I could not read ~~his~~my own work without feeling slightly nauseous.

Later, looking through the manuscript, I touched a page and found the paper slick with the slime of spit. When my father did his National Service in Egypt, one of his duties was to serve his officer tea in bed in the morning. Before adding the hot water, my father would spit in the mug. Now, reading over the words that were worthy of derision, I picked up the wad of paper and placed it warily in the recycling bin.

Began again.

Fresh clean pages~~ and the writer's father collapsing.~~

Only this time, instead of spitting on them, my father collapsed on them, folded to the floor and ~~resting~~rested there, damaged, the blood leaking out into his brain for three treacherous hours. 5 February 1989. After the stroke ~~the writer's father~~ he lost the power of language~~, he~~. He stared out from the dumb pages, frustrated and in pain.

When ~~the writer~~I tried to move him from one page to the other ~~he~~I discovered that ~~the man~~he could barely limp through the narrative.

~~And so, beginning at~~I began again. At the end~~, the writer chose~~ this time, desperate for a circling narrative. The last conversation ~~between the writer and his father.~~I had with him: 18 March 2012. ~~The writer~~I recorded each sentence, word by word, and yet when ~~he~~I read back over the work ~~he discovered there was no content, no meaning. The~~the words were barely recognisable, providing no meaning and no context. ~~More~~ Nothing but more paper for the recycling bin.

~~He flirted with the idea of~~More desperation. I tried a mystery in which ~~the writer kills his father~~I killed him by fracturing his skull with an encyclopaedia. Freud nodded his sage head~~. Free~~ as, free of the spectre of ~~his~~my father, ~~the writer~~I was now free to make passionate love to ~~his~~my mother. ~~The writer~~I reached for her brassiere~~. The writer~~, then stopped~~,~~. Ludicrous. I tore up the offending page.

~~In desperation, he decided to shake off the shackles of the real world and try~~I tried fantasy. ~~All the wrongs of their relationship could be righted.~~ Typing the words~~,~~: 'My father often told me that he loved me' would make them true. ~~He~~I typed ~~the words~~them and ~~his~~my father spoke them, but the corner of his mouth turned upward in a sneer~~ and the words were damaged by his~~. The inflection was all wrong.

~~His~~My father needed an easier life. He needed joy. ~~The writer~~I rewrote his ~~father's~~ childhood. ~~Removing~~I removed the boy who used to beat him up each afternoon after school. ~~He~~I invented a long and lovely romance for ~~his parents,~~him and my mother, with a wedding dress for ~~his mother~~her that was tight about her waist because in this version of her life she was not already pregnant. ~~He~~Godlike, I cleared the blockage in ~~his~~my father's brain and blessed his future with language. In this new, forgiving narrative ~~his~~my father published books, became a celebrated author. ~~The writer~~I stood in line at his ~~father's~~ book launch~~. He~~, my copy of his book pressed ~~the book~~ open to the title page. *To my son*, wrote ~~his~~my father~~, pausing. The writer~~. There was a pause.

I was in charge of the story. ~~The writer~~I held ~~his~~my father's pen. *With love*. ~~The writer~~I made the marks on the page, but when ~~the~~my father pushed the book across the signing table there was an ironic underline under the word *love*. There were little hearts and crosses. ~~His~~My father grinned like a manic cherub. ~~The writer~~I glanced down to see the edges of the heart dissolving. ~~His father~~He had, yet again, spat on the page.

One afternoon last year, ~~the writer~~I had an epiphany while sitting in a crowded waiting room for an hour and a half before ~~he~~I could see a doctor. ~~He soon~~I had finished the novel ~~he~~I was reading, and all the magazines were already taken, so for something to read ~~he~~I picked a pamphlet at random from a plastic rack on the wall. When ~~he~~I finished it, ~~he~~I realised that ~~his~~my father had been depressed for most of his adult life. And so, it turned out, had ~~he~~I. That night ~~he~~I went to bed early and was in that state between waking and dreaming when your mind does strange things. ~~He~~I was drifting, thinking about how it would be breakfast time in Scotland, the hour that ~~his~~my father used to call, on the rare occasions that he did. And then ~~the writer's~~my phone started ringing at the other end of ~~his~~my house.

~~He~~I scrambled out of bed~~. He~~, then stopped. ~~He~~I could see ~~his~~my father standing in the hallway of his house in Scotland, the phone pressed to his ear. The phone switched on to the answering machine just before ~~the writer~~I could reach it.

'Hello?' ~~he~~I heard ~~his~~my father say~~.~~, 'Hello?'

~~My Father as a Short Story by Cate Kennedy~~

I started logically, or tried to. My father, born on the third floor of the tenement building in the east end of Glasgow, on 20 July 1935. I wrote these words then felt the story fall fatally silent. I put my hand on the baby's chest and found there was no breath in him. A father still-born.

I began again. St Bridget's chapel in Edinburgh, where my father and mother were married on 3 August 1971. Words raining down on the blank pages with the dry rustle of thrown rice. Over the next three days the rice swelled. A blue mould set in, changing the scent of the words. I could not read my own work without feeling slightly nauseous.

Later, looking through the manuscript, I touched a page and found the paper slick with the slime of spit. When my father did his National Service in Egypt, one of his duties was to serve his officer tea in bed in the morning. Before adding the hot water, my father would spit in the mug. Now, reading over the words that were worthy of derision, I picked up the wad of paper and placed it warily in the recycling bin.

Began again.

Fresh clean pages.

Only this time, instead of spitting on them, my father collapsed on them, folded to the floor and rested there, damaged, the blood leaking out into his brain for three treacherous hours. 5 February 1989. After the stroke he lost the power of language. He stared out from the dumb pages, frustrated and in pain. When I tried to move him from one page to the other I discovered that he could barely limp through the narrative.

I began again. At the end this time, desperate for a circling narrative. The last conversation I had with him: 18 March 2012. I recorded each sentence, word by word, and yet when I read back over the work the words were barely recognisable, providing no meaning and no context.

Nothing but more paper for the recycling bin.

More desperation. I tried a mystery in which I killed him by fracturing his skull with an encyclopaedia. Freud nodded his sage head as, free of the spectre of my father, I was now free to make passionate love to my mother. I reached for her brassiere, then stopped. Ludicrous. I tore up the offending page.

I tried fantasy. Typing the words: 'My father often told me that he loved me' would make them true. I typed them and my father spoke them, but the corner of his mouth turned upward in a sneer. The inflection was all wrong.

My father needed an easier life. He needed joy. I rewrote his childhood. I removed the boy who used to beat him up each afternoon after school. I invented a long and lovely romance for him and my mother, with a wedding dress for her that was tight about her waist because in this version of her life she was not already pregnant. Godlike, I cleared the blockage in my father's brain and blessed his future with language. In this new, forgiving narrative my father published books, became a celebrated author. I stood in line at his book launch, my copy of his book pressed open to the title page. To my son, wrote my father. There was a pause.

I was in charge of the story. I held my father's pen. With love. I made the marks on the page, but when my father pushed the book across the signing table there was an ironic underline under the word love. There were little hearts and crosses. My father grinned like a manic cherub. I glanced down to see the edges of the heart dissolving. He had, yet again, spat on the page.

One afternoon last year, I had an epiphany while sitting in a crowded waiting room for an hour and a half before I could see a doctor. I had finished the novel I was reading, and all the magazines were already taken, so for something to read I picked a pamphlet at random from a plastic rack on the wall. When I finished it, I realised that my father had been depressed for most of his adult life. And so, it turned out, had I.

That night I went to bed early and was in that state between waking and dreaming when your mind does strange things. I was drifting, thinking about how it would be breakfast time in Scotland, the hour that my father used to call, on the rare occasions that he did. And then my phone started ringing at the other end of my house.

I scrambled out of bed, then stopped. I could see my father standing in the hallway of his house in Scotland, the phone pressed to his ear.

The phone switched on to the answering machine just before I could reach it.

‘Hello?’ I heard my father say, ‘Hello?’

My Father as a Short Story

Well, you'll make up your own mind, so I ~~started~~may as well just tell it. The words are the words; the truth—as almost always—is woven between them; not from them. But hear this: none of this is true, except the start and the ending.
Starting logically~~, or tried to. My~~: my father, born July 20, 1935 on the third floor of the tenement building in the east end of Glasgow~~, on 20 July 1935. I wrote these~~. The words ~~then felt~~written, the story ~~fall~~falls fatally silent. I put my hand ~~on~~to the baby's chest and found ~~there was~~ no breath in him. A father, dead still; still-born.
~~I began again.~~Starting in faith: St Bridget's chapel~~ in~~, Edinburgh, where my father and mother ~~were~~ married on ~~3~~ August 3, 1971. Words raining down on the blank pages with the dry rustle of thrown rice. Over the next three days the rice swelled. A blue mould set~~ in~~, changing the scent of the words. I could not read my ~~own~~ work without feeling slightly nauseous. Sickened by sentences, lost in a language that does not feel my own.
~~Later~~Starting abroad: later, looking through the manuscript, I touched a page and found the paper slick with the slime of spit. When my father did his National Service in Egypt, one of his duties was to serve his officer tea in bed in the morning. Before adding the hot water, my father would spit in the mug. This part I know to be true. I saw him do it once to a neighbour, who had asked to borrow father's axe, then used it to dig rocks from the grass. Now, reading over the words that were worthy of derision, I picked up the wad of paper and placed it warily in the recycling bin.
~~Began again.~~
~~Fresh clean pages.~~
~~Only~~Starting afresh.
Starting on the page: this time, instead of spitting on them, my father collapsed on them, folded to the floor and rested there, damaged, the blood leaking out into his brain for three treacherous hours. 5 February 1989. After the stroke he lost ~~the power of~~ language. It was stolen from him, replaced by a limp. He stared out from the dumb pages, frustrated~~ and~~, in pain. When I tried to move him from one page to the other I discovered~~ that~~ he could barely limp through the narrative.
~~I began~~Starting again~~. At~~: at the end this time, desperate for a ~~circling narrative~~ story circle. The last conversation I had with him: ~~18~~ March 18, 2012. I recorded each sentence, word ~~by~~for word, and yet when I read back over the work the words were barely recognisable~~, providing~~ —no meaning and no context. Syllables without sense. ~~Nothing but more paper for the recycling bin.~~
~~More desperation. I tried a~~ Ending in mystery: I wrote a life as a crime, a story in which I killed him by fracturing his skull with an encyclopaedia. Freud nodded his sage head as, free of the spectre of my father, I was now free to make passionate love to my mother. I reached for her brassiere, then stopped. Ludicrous. I tore up the offending page.
~~I tried~~Ending in fantasy~~. Typing~~: typing the words: 'My father often told me that he loved me' would make them true. I typed them and my father spoke them, but the corner of his mouth turned upward in a sneer. The inflection was all wrong.
~~My~~Ending at the beginning: my father needed an easier life. He needed joy. I rewrote his childhood. I removed the boy who used to beat him up each afternoon after school. I invented a long ~~and~~, lovely romance for him and my mother, with a wedding dress for her that was tight about her waist because in this version of her life she was not already pregnant. Godlike, I cleared the blockage in my father's brain and blessed his future with language. In this ~~new,~~ forgiving narrative my father published books, became a celebrated author. I stood in line at his book launch, my copy of his book pressed open to the title page. *To my son*, wrote my father. There was a pause.
~~I was~~Ending in in charge~~ of the story.~~: I held my father's pen. *With love*. I made the marks on the page, but when my father pushed the book across the signing table there was an ironic underline under the word *love*. There were little hearts and crosses. My father grinned like a manic cherub. I glanced down to see the edges of the heart dissolving. ~~He had, yet again,~~Again, he spat on the page.
~~One~~Ending in revelation: one afternoon last year, I had an epiphany ~~while sitting~~stuck in a crowded waiting room for an hour and a half before I could see

a doctor. I had finished the novel I was reading, and all the magazines were already taken, so for something to read I picked a pamphlet at random from a plastic rack on the wall. When I finished it, I realised that my father had been depressed for most of his adult life. And so, it turned out, had I.

~~That~~ The truth: that night I went to bed early ~~and was in that state between waking and dreaming when your mind does strange things.~~. The edge of sleep rushed towards me but I did not fall over. I was drifting, thinking about how it would be breakfast ~~time~~ in Scotland, the hour ~~that~~ my father used to call, on the rare occasions that he did. And then my phone started ringing at the other end of my house.

I scrambled out of bed, then stopped. I could see ~~my father standing~~him there in the hallway of his house in Scotland, the phone pressed to his ear.

The phone switched on to the answering machine just before I could reach it.

'Hello?' I heard my father say, 'Hello?'

These are the words I wrote down.

All of this is true except the start and the ending.

~~My Father as a Short Story by Robert Hoge~~

Well, you'll make up your own mind, so I may as well just tell it. The words are the words; the truth – as almost always – is woven between them; not from them. But hear this: none of this is true, except the start and the ending.

Starting logically: my father, born July 20, 1935 on the third floor of the tenement building in the east end of Glasgow. The words written, the story falls fatally silent. I put my hand to the baby's chest and found no breath in him. A father, dead still; still-born.

Starting in faith: St Bridget's chapel, Edinburgh, where my father and mother married on August 3, 1971. Words raining down on the blank pages with the dry rustle of thrown rice. Over the next three days the rice swelled. A blue mould set, changing the scent of the words. I could not read my work without feeling slightly nauseous. Sickened by sentences, lost in a language that does not feel my own.

Starting abroad: later, looking through the manuscript, I touched a page and found the paper slick with the slime of spit. When my father did his National Service in Egypt, one of his duties was to serve his officer tea in bed in the morning. Before adding the hot water, my father would spit in the mug. This part I know to be true. I saw him do it once to a neighbour, who had asked to borrow father's axe, then used it to dig rocks from the grass. Now, reading over the words that were worthy of derision, I picked up the wad of paper and placed it warily in the recycling bin.

Starting afresh.

Starting on the page: this time, instead of spitting on them, my father collapsed on them, folded to the floor and rested there, damaged, the blood leaking out into his brain for three treacherous hours. February 5, 1989. After the stroke he lost language. It was stolen from him, replaced by a limp. He stared out from the dumb pages, frustrated; in pain. When I tried to move him from one page to the other I discovered he could barely limp through the narrative.

Starting again: at the end this time, desperate for a story circle. The last conversation I had with him: March 18, 2012. I recorded each sentence, word for word, and yet, when I read back over the work, the words were barely recognisable – no meaning and no context. Syllables without sense.

Ending in mystery: I wrote a life as a crime, a story in which I killed him by fracturing his skull with an encyclopaedia. Freud nodded his sage head as, free of the spectre of my father, I was now free to make passionate love to my mother. I reached for her brassiere, then stopped. Ludicrous. I tore up the offending page.

Ending in fantasy: typing the words: 'My father often told me that he loved me' would make them true. I typed them and my father spoke them, but the corner of his mouth turned upward in a sneer. The inflection was all wrong.

Ending at the beginning: my father needed an easier life. He needed joy. I rewrote his childhood. I removed the boy who used to beat him up each afternoon after school. I invented a long, lovely romance for him and my mother, with a wedding dress for her that was tight about her waist because in this version of her life she was not already pregnant. Godlike, I cleared the blockage in my father's brain and blessed his future with language. In this forgiving narrative my father published books, became a celebrated author. I stood in line at his book launch, my copy of his book pressed open to the title page. To my son, wrote my father. There was a pause.

Ending in in charge: I held my father's pen. With love. I made the marks on the page, but when my father pushed the book across the signing table there was an ironic underline under the word love. There were little hearts and crosses. My father grinned like a manic cherub. I glanced down to see the edges of the heart dissolving. Again, he spat on the page.

Ending in revelation: one afternoon last year, I had an epiphany stuck in a crowded waiting room for an hour and a half before I could see a doctor. I had finished the novel I was reading, and all the magazines were already taken, so for something to read I picked a pamphlet at random from a plastic rack on the wall. When I finished it, I realised that my father had been depressed for most of his adult life. And so, it turned out, had I.

The truth: that night I went to bed early. The edge of sleep rushed towards me but I did not fall over. I was drifting, thinking about how it would be breakfast in Scotland, the hour my father used to call, on the rare occasions that he did. And then my phone started ringing at the other end of my house. I scrambled out of bed, then stopped. I could see him there in the hallway of his house in Scotland, the phone pressed to his ear. The phone switched on to the answering machine just before I could reach it.

'Hello?' I heard my father say, 'Hello?'

These are the words I wrote down.

All of this is true except the start and the ending.

~~Cyclone Dragitsa by Krissy Kneen~~

The tap will not stop dripping. The enamel is discoloured, light green, a deeper blue at the centre of the stain. A scab of salt on the scrubbed white of the bowl. I frown at the wound briefly. It is the result of hard water pumped up from an underground bore.

I remember bathing myself in a bucket of rainwater drawn down from the tank. The rest of them could use the shower. There were six of us then, two from each generation. There was a kind of balance to it but I was not to know it way back then. In winter I would shiver between handfuls of warmth. The water was heated on the stove but it would cool too quickly. I was always sticky with a fine layer of soap still clinging to my skin after the sponge bath. My hair was lank. I was jealous of my sister, my mother, my grandmother, all of them stepping lightly from a shower, pinked with the heat of it, clean and sweet with suds. There was nothing to be done. My skin would rebel against the ground-water. My arms flushed red, my chest flared in patches. Naked and weeping in my bedroom I would dab at the spots with calamine lotion, replacing the red patches with splotches of white.

There was never a mirror in our house, which was lucky because I might have been turned to stone, transfixed by the sight of my own skin rebelling against this poisonous landscape.

My grandmother never allowed mirrors. She would never approve of all these mirrors crammed into one tiny motel room. There is a full-length mirror in the bedroom, a mirror on the inside of the cupboard door, another above the sink throwing my own face back at me. I look pale and overblown. My skin is damp with a sheen of sweat. My nightmares have punched me in both eyes and there is a shadow of a fist mark above each cheek. I may have put on weight. She would have noticed. She would have told me I needed to diet.

I put her on the ceramic of the sink. She is heavy, silent. They have clothed her in a red velveteen bag with a gold pull cord as if this is a theatre. I can imagine her climbing out of the plastic container, pulling the cord. Ta Da! She is a magician and she reassembles herself in a puff of smoke.

I fear and long for this in equal measure.

I am glad she is gone. I am sad she is gone. I am certain that now, at the death-end of things she will come back to take us all out with her.

There is a cyclone approaching the coast up north, a battlefield of the dead rotting in its wake. This is not of her doing, and yet it is also her hand at work. She used to crack walnuts in one trembling fist. She was mighty and she will cross the coast at Cairns tomorrow morning or perhaps by lunchtime.

I must put her in the ground before she wreaks havoc, warms the globe, raises tide-lines and steals whole continents.

There is a raised red patch of skin on my neck. I showered when I arrived here. I put her ashes down on the bed and stepped under the crusted shower rose and bathed my body in the harsh water knowing what would happen if I did.

'Did we bring the allergy stuff?' I say.

'What allergy stuff?' He says.

'You know the tablets?'

I can hear my husband searching in the overnight bag, the crinkle of a blister pack.

'Nexium?'

'No.'

'What's it called?'

'Fexo-something? It will say anti-histamine on it somewhere.'

The soft wamp of clothes falling to the carpet.

'No. We could go to the chemist.'

'There isn't one. Or there is, but an hour away.'

I scratch at my neck and my nails leave fine red lines.

'Will you be ok?'

I nod. He couldn't see, but I hear some music, voices. He is watching something on his phone.

The lid of the plastic vessel has a circle in the top. The woman who handed it to me at the funeral place told me to pop it off with a knife. There is no knife. I push at it with the rounded end of a teaspoon. It's tight. It seems like it might be sealed shut.

I can hear two people talking in the next room along. A voice raised, a woman's voice. Then softer, a man. They are having an argument. I stop and listen but it is just the drone of voices like two bees trapped in a bottle.

I lift my grandmother and shake her. She sounds like a tub of sand.

Outside the rain starts up. On the long ride up here we were racing into it. Dark clouds, distant, then closer. Driving back down to Miriam Vale from the funeral place in Gladstone the clouds began to chase us.

'That's that cyclone.' my husband said, 'or the beginning of it.'

'Cyclone Dragitsa' I said, invoking her name, and he laughed, nodding in agreement.

The rain is sudden and hard. It drowns out the argument next door despite its escalation. I wish they would stop. Don't they know that nothing matters? I know it now. Really know it. Nothing matters, not their yelling, or the coming cyclone or whatever petty little detail caused the neighbour's fury. Nothing matters because I am holding her in my hands and she is both too heavy and too light.

I turn the spoon around, worry the circle with the thinner bent end of it. The seal pops. I prise and it comes off entirely. I look inside and it isn't sand, it is courser, and, strangely, a pinking grey in colour. It looks exactly like the kitty litter we used to buy from Coles before our cat was killed on the road. It looks synthetic, a chemical reek. There is nothing of my grandmother in here. Still, I pour a small measure into a small plastic vial. I dip my finger in, touch it, pick a pinch of stones (bones) up between my thumb and forefinger. I place it on my tongue. I swallow.

The wind picks up, howls. The corrugated awning outside the motel room rattles violently. The people arguing next door are silenced by the sound of it. We are all a hush.

'Are you ok in there?' The sound of my husband's voice.

I nod, again.

'That storm's going to be a beauty,' he says.

I have to get her in the ground.

Cyclone Dragitsa

Category One Cyclone

First person narrators begin to show signs of unreliability.
Some instability may be expected in the present tense.
Verbs, and occasionally adjectives, become prone to tautology.
However, a well-constructed story will suffer no substantial structural damage.

The tap will not stop dripping, dribbling, leaking, splashing, plopping. The enamel is discoloured, light green, a deeper blue at the centre of the stain. A scab of salt on the scrubbed white of the bowl. (All this took place many years ago, and yet I ~~frown~~remember such small details with perfect clarity. Don't you recall the exact colour of the basins in the motel rooms you have stayed in throughout your life?) I scowl, frowned, glare at the wound briefly. It is the result of hard water pumped up, driven, forced, pushed, transported, from an underground bore.

I remember bathing and washing myself in a bucket of rainwater drawn and extracted down from the tank. The rest of them could use and take the shower. There ~~were~~are six of us then, two from each generation. There was a kind of balance to it that you usually only find in stories, but I was not to know ~~it~~or comprehend that way back then. In winter I would shiver, tremble, shake, quiver between handfuls of warmth. The water was heated and boiled on the stove but it would cool and become less hot too quickly. I was always sticky (or was it gummy?) with a fine layer of soap still clinging, adhering and gluing to my skin after the sponge bath. My hair was lank~~.~~, lustreless, limp, lifeless. I was jealous of my sister, my mother, my grandmother, all of them stepping and prancing lightly from a shower, pinked with the heat of it, clean and sweet with suds. There ~~was~~is nothing to be done. My skin would rebel and revolt against the ground-water. My arms flushed and blushed red, my chest ~~flared~~flares, blazes, flashes in patches. Naked, without clothes and weeping and shedding tears in my bedroom I would dab and pat and blot and mop at the spots with calamine lotion, replacing, swapping the red patches with splotches of white.

Category Two Cyclone

Words are peeled from the page, revealing the lexical category beneath.
Longer sentences may be snapped in two, or uprooted.
Adjectives can come loose from their moorings and be blown across the page.
The story begins to show signs of structural damage

There was never a ~~mirror~~noun in our house, which was lucky because I might have been turned to stone, transfixed by the sight of my own skin ~~rebelling.~~ Rebelling against this poisonous landscape.

pale

My grandmother never allowed ~~mirrors~~nouns. She would never approve of all these ~~mirrors~~nouns crammed into one tiny motel room. There is a full-length ~~mirror~~noun in the bedroom, a ~~mirror~~noun on the inside ~~of~~. Of the cupboard door, another above the sink throwing ~~my~~. My own face back at me. I look ~~pale~~ and overblown. My skin is ~~damp~~ with a sheen of sweat. My nightmares have ~~punched~~verbed me in both eyes and there is a shadow of a fist mark above each cheek. I ~~may~~modal verb have put on weight. She would have noticed. She would have told me I needed to ~~diet~~ verb. damp

I put her on the ceramic of the sink. She is heavy, ~~silent~~ . They have clothed her in a red ~~velveteen~~ bag with a gold pull cord as if this is a theatre. I can imagine her climbing out of ~~the~~definite article plastic container, pulling the cord. ~~Ta Da~~Interjection! She is a magician and she ~~reassembles~~. Reassembles herself in a puff of smoke.

velveteen

Silent

sad

glad

I fear and long for this in equal measure. I am ~~glad~~ she is gone. I am ~~sad~~ she is gone. I am certain that now, at the death-end of things she will come back to take us all out with her.

Category Three Cyclone

Text alignment breaks down.
The story is flooded with clichés, leaving areas of the narrative isolated.
Extensive erosion of dialogue.
The story shows signs of serious structural damage.

There is a cyclone ~~approaching~~coming like a bat out of hell from the coast up north, a battlefield of the dead, wake up and smell the coffee, and the rotting in its wake. Still, every cloud has a silver lining. This is not of her doing, and yet it is also her hand at work. She used to crack walnuts in one trembling fist~~.~~, strong as an ox, she was. She ~~was mighty and she~~ will cross the coast like an avenging angel at Cairns tomorrow morning or perhaps by lunchtime~~.~~, proving there is no such thing as a free lunch.

I must put her in the ground before she wreaks havoc, warms the globe, raises tide-lines and steals whole continents~~.~~ out of the frying pan and into the fire.

There is a raised red patch of skin on my otherwise flawless, bronzed neck. I showered clean as a whistle when I arrived here. I put her ashes to ashes, dust to dust down on the bed and stepped under the crusted shower rose and bathed my body in the harsh water knowing what would happen if I did.

'Did we bring ~~the allergy~~.......... stuff?' I say.

'What allergy ~~stuff?~~.........?' He says.

'You ~~know~~......... the ~~tablets?~~............?'

I can hear my ~~husband~~other half searching in the overnight bag, the crinkle of a blister pack.

~~'Nexium?'~~...............?'

'No.'

'What's ~~it~~...... called?'

'Fexo-~~something?~~s................? It will say anti-histamine ~~on it~~........... somewhere.'

The soft wamp of clothes falling to the carpet.

'No. ~~We~~............could go to the chemist.'

~~'There isn't one.'~~............... Or there is, but an hour away.'

I scratch ~~at~~ my ~~neck~~back (and you scratch yours) and my nails leave fine red lines.

~~'Will you be ok?'~~...................?

I give a wink and a nod. He couldn't see, but I hear some music, voices. He is ~~watching something on~~ glued to his phone.

Category Four Cyclone

Large areas of the text are flattened.

Irreparable damage to paragraph structure.

Sentences are carried a considerable distance.

Extensive structural damage to the story

The lid of the plastic vessel has a circle in the

top. The woman who handed it to me at

____

___________the funeral place told me to pop it off with a knife.

There is no knife. I push at it with the

rounded end of a teaspoon. It's tight. It seems like it might be sealed shut.

I can hear two people talking

in the next room along. A voice raised, a woman's

voice. Then softer, a man. They are having an argument. I stop and listen but it is just the drone of voices ~~like two bees trapped in a bottle.~~

like two bees trapped in a bottle.

I lift my grandmother and shake her.

She sounds like a tub of sand.

____

____

___________Outside the rain starts up. On the

long ride up here we were racing into it. Dark clouds, distant, then closer. Driving

back down to Miriam Vale from the

funeral place in Gladstone the clouds began to chase us.

'That's that cyclone.' my

husband said, 'or the beginning of it.'

'__________________________________

___________Cyclone Dragitsa' I said,

invoking her name, and he laughed, nodding

in agreement.

~~The rain is sudden and hard. It drowns out the argument next door despite its escalation. I wish they would stop. Don't they know that nothing matters? I know it now. Really know it. Nothing matters, not their yelling, or the coming cyclone or whatever petty little detail caused the neighbour's fury. Nothing matters because I am holding her in my hands~~

~~Cyclone Dragitsa by Ryan O'Neill~~

Category One Cyclone

First person narrators begin to show signs of unreliability. Some instability may be expected in the present tense. Verbs, and occasionally adjectives, become prone to tautology. However, a well-constructed story will suffer no substantial structural damage.

The tap will not stop dripping, dribbling, leaking, splashing, plopping. The enamel is discoloured, light green, a deeper blue at the centre of the stain. A scab of salt on the scrubbed white of the bowl. (All this took place many years ago, and yet I remember such small details with perfect clarity. Don't you recall the exact colour of the basins in the motel rooms you have stayed in throughout your life?) I scowl, frowned, glare at the wound briefly. It is the result of hard water pumped up, driven, forced, pushed, transported, from an underground bore.

I remember bathing and washing myself in a bucket of rainwater drawn and extracted down from the tank. The rest of them could use and take the shower. There are six of us then, two from each generation. There was a kind of balance to it that you usually only find in stories, but I was not to know or comprehend that way back then. In winter I would shiver, tremble, shake, quiver between handfuls of warmth. The water was heated and boiled on the stove but it would cool and become less hot too quickly. I was always sticky (or was it gummy?) with a fine layer of soap still clinging, adhering and gluing to my skin after the sponge bath. My hair was lank, lustreless, limp, lifeless. I was jealous of my sister, my mother, my grandmother, all of them stepping and prancing lightly from a shower, pinked with the heat of it, clean and sweet with suds. There is nothing to be done. My skin would rebel and revolt against the ground-water. My arms flushed and blushed red, my chest flares, blazes, flashes in patches. Naked, without clothes and weeping and shedding tears in my bedroom I would dab and pat and blot and mop at the spots with calamine lotion, replacing, swapping the red patches with splotches of white.

Category Two Cyclone

Words are peeled from the page, revealing the lexical category beneath. Longer sentences may be snapped in two, or uprooted. Adjectives can come loose from their moorings and be blown across the page. The story begins to show signs of structural damage.

There was never a noun in our house, which was lucky because I might have been turned to stone, transfixed by the sight of my own skin. Rebelling against this poisonous landscape.

pale

My grandmother never allowed nouns. She would never approve of all these nouns crammed into one tiny motel room. There is a full-length noun in the bedroom, a noun on the inside. Of the cupboard door, another above the sink throwing. My own face back at me. I look …… and overblown. My skin is …… with a sheen of sweat. My nightmares have verbed me in both eyes and there is a shadow of a fist mark above each cheek. I modal verb have put on weight. She would have noticed. She would have told me I needed to verb.

damp

I put her on the ceramic of the sink. She is heavy, ……. They have clothed her in a red …… bag with a gold pull cord as if this is a theatre. I can imagine her climbing out of definite article plastic container, pulling the cord. Interjection! She is a magician and she. Reassembles herself in a puff of smoke.

velveteen

Silent

sad

glad

I fear and long for this in equal measure.

I am … she is gone. I am … she is gone. I am certain that now, at the death-end of things she will come back to take us all out with her.

Category Three Cyclone

Text alignment breaks down. The story is flooded with clichés, leaving areas of the narrative isolated. Extensive erosion of dialogue. The story shows signs of serious structural damage.

There is a cyclone coming like a bat out of hell from the coast up north, a battlefield of the dead; wake up and smell the coffee, and the rotting in its wake. Still, every cloud has a silver lining. This is not of her doing, and yet it is also her hand at work. She used to crack walnuts in one trembling fist, strong as an ox, she was. She will cross the coast like an avenging angel at Cairns tomorrow morning or perhaps by lunchtime, proving there is no such thing as a free lunch.

I must put her in the ground before she wreaks havoc, warms the globe, raises tide-lines and steals whole continents out of the frying pan and into the fire.

There is a raised red patch of skin on my otherwise flawless, bronzed neck. I showered clean as a whistle when I arrived here. I put her ashes to ashes, dust to dust down on the bed and stepped under the crusted shower rose and bathed my body in the harsh water knowing what would happen if I did.

'Did we bring…......... stuff?' I say.

'What allergy ……….?' He says.

'You ………. the …………?'

I can hear my other half searching in the overnight bag, the crinkle of a blister pack.

'……………..?'

'No.'

'What's ……. called?'

'Fexo-s………………? It will say anti-histamine

………….. somewhere.'

The soft wamp of clothes falling to the carpet.

'No. …………..could go to the chemist.'

'……………... Or there is, but an hour away.'

I scratch my back
(and you scratch yours)
and my nails leave fine
red lines.

'…………………?'

I give a wink and a nod. He couldn't see,
but I hear some music, voices. He is glued to
his phone.

Category Four Cyclone

Large areas of the text are flattened. Irreparable damage to paragraph structure. Sentences are carried a considerable distance. Extensive structural damage to the story.

The lid of the plastic vessel has a circle in the

top. The woman who handed it to me at
the funeral place told me to pop it off with a knife.
There is no knife. I push at it with the

rounded end of a **teaspoon. It's**
tight. It *seems like it might* be sealed
shut.

I can hear two people talking

in the *next room along.* ***A voice raised, a woman's***
voice. Then softer, a man. They are having an argument. I
stop and lis***ten but it is just* the drone *of voices***

like two **bees trapped** ***in a bottle.***

I lift my grandmot her ***and shake her.***

She sounds like **a tub of sand.**

Outside the rain starts up. On

the

long ride up here we

were racing into it.

Dark clouds, distant, then closer.

Driving

back down to Miriam Vale ***from the***

funeral place in **G**ladst**one the clouds began to chase**

us.

'That's that cyclone.' my

husband said, 'or the ginning of it.'

' Cyclone Dragitsa' I said,

invoking her name, he laughed, nodding

in agreement.

Category Five Cyclone

Absolute destruction of the story.

The rain is sudden and hard. It drowns out the argument next door despite its escalation. I wish they would stop. Don't they know that nothing matters? I know it now. Really know it. Nothing matters, not their yelling, it.

I turn the spoon around, worry the with the thinner bent end of it. The seal pops. I prise and it comes off entirely. I look inside and it isn't sand, it courser, and strangely, a pinkish grey in colour.

the spoon around, worry
le with the thinner bent
t. The seal pops. I prise and
off entirely. I look
ide and it
t sand, it
courser

was killed on the road. It looks synthetic, a chemical reek. There is nothing of my grandmother in here. Still, I pour a small measure into a small plastic vial.

'ARE YOU OK IN THERE?' The sound of my husband's voice.

I nod, again.

'THAT STORM'S GOING TO BE A BEAUTY,' he says.

I have to get her in the ground.

There is a cyclone coming like a bat out of hell from the coast up north, a battlefield left in its wake.

Outside the rain starts up. On the long ride up here we were racing into it. Dark clouds, distant, then closer. ~~***Category One Cyclone***~~

~~First person narrators begin to show signs of unreliability.~~
~~Some instability may be expected in the present tense.~~
~~Verbs, and occasionally adjectives, become prone to tautology.~~
~~However, a well-constructed story will suffer no substantial structural damage.~~

Driving back down to Miriam Vale from the funeral place in Gladstone the clouds had begun to chase us.
'That's that cyclone,' my husband said, 'or the beginning of it.'
'Cyclone Dragitsa' I said, invoking her name, and he laughed, nodding in agreement.
I must put her in the ground before she wreaks havoc.

The tap will not stop dripping~~, dribbling, leaking, splashing, plopping. The~~ and the enamel is discoloured, light green, a deeper blue at the centre of the stain. A scab of salt on the scrubbed white of the bowl. ~~(All this took place many years ago, and yet I remember such small details with perfect clarity. Don't you recall the exact colour of the basins in the motel rooms you have stayed in throughout your life?) I scowl, frowned, glare at the wound briefly. It is the result of hard water pumped up, driven, forced, pushed, transported, from an underground bore.~~
~~I remember bathing and washing~~I showered when I arrived here at the motel. I put her ashes down on the ceramic sink and stepped under the crusted shower rose and bathed my body in the harsh bore water knowing what would happen if I did.
As a child I would wash myself in a bucket of rainwater drawn ~~and extracted down~~ from the tank. ~~The rest of them could use and take the shower. There are six of us then, two from each generation. There was a kind of balance to it that you usually only find in stories, but I was not to know or comprehend that way back then.~~ In winter I would shiver~~, tremble, shake, quiver~~ between handfuls of warmth~~. The~~ from water that was heated ~~and boiled~~ on the stove but ~~it would cool and become less hot~~always cooled too quickly. ~~I was always sticky (or was it gummy?) with a fine layer of soap still clinging, adhering and gluing to my skin after the sponge~~ bath. My hair was lank~~, lustreless,~~ and limp~~, lifeless~~ with residual soap. I was jealous of my sister, my mother, my grandmother~~,~~ —all of them stepping ~~and prancing~~ lightly from a shower, pinked with the heat of it, clean and sweet with suds. ~~There is nothing to be done. My~~But my skin would rebel ~~and revolt~~ against the ~~ground-water. My~~ hard groundwater; my arms ~~flushed and blushed~~flushing red, my chest ~~flares, blazes, flashes in patches.~~flaring, itching. Naked~~, without clothes~~ and weeping ~~and shedding tears~~ in my bedroom I would dab ~~and pat and blot and mop~~ at the spots with calamine lotion, replacing~~, swapping~~ the red patches with splotches of white.

~~***Category Two Cyclone***~~
~~*Words are peeled from the page, revealing the lexical category beneath.*~~
~~*Longer sentences may be snapped in two, or uprooted.*~~
~~*Adjectives can come loose from their moorings and be blown across the page.*~~
~~*The story begins to show signs of structural damage*~~

There was never a ~~noun~~mirror in our house~~,~~ - which was lucky because I might have been turned to stone~~, transfixed~~ by the sight of my own skin~~. Rebelling against this poisonous landscape.~~

~~pale~~
~~My~~ – and my grandmother never allowed ~~nouns~~them. She would never approve of all these ~~nouns~~mirrors crammed into one tiny motel room~~.~~ ~~There is a~~; the full-length ~~noun~~one in the bedroom, ~~a noun~~the one on the inside~~.~~ ~~Of~~ of the cupboard door~~, another above the sink throwing. My own face back at me. I look and overblown. My skin is with a sheen of sweat. My nightmares have verbed me in both eyes and there is a shadow of a fist mark above each cheek. I modal verb have put on weight. She would have noticed. She would have told me I needed to verb. damp~~.
And this one above the sink, throwing my own face back at me, sheened with sweat. I look damp and overblown. There is a raised red patch of skin on my neck.

'Did we bring any skin allergy stuff?' I call to my husband.
'What's it called?'
'In a blister pack. It'll say antihistamine somewhere.'
I hear him searching; clothes falling to the carpet.
'No, but I could go to the chemist.'
'There's no chemist. Or there is, but an hour away.'
I scratch my back and my nails leave fine red lines.
He is glued to his phone. I can hear him talking.

I lift ~~I put her on the ceramic of the sink. She is heavy,~~ my grandmother from the sink, and shake her. She sounds like a tub of sand. They have clothed her in a red velveteen bag with a gold pull cord, as if this is ~~a~~ theatre. I ~~can~~ imagine her climbing out of ~~definite article plastic~~ the container, pulling the cord ~~Interjection! She is~~ like a magician ~~and she. Reassembles~~, Reassembling herself in a puff of smoke.~~————————~~
~~———————— velveteen~~
~~Silent ————————~~
~~sad ————————~~
~~glad~~
I ~~fear and~~ long for and fear this in equal measure.
~~I am she is gone. I am she is gone. I am certain that now, at the death-end of things she will come back to take us all out with her.~~

~~***Category Three Cyclone***~~

~~Text~~
~~alignmen~~
~~t breaks~~
~~down.~~

~~The *story is flooded with clichés, leaving areas of the narrative isolated.*~~
~~*Extensive erosion of dialogue.*~~
~~*The story shows signs of serious structural damage.*~~

~~There is a cyclone coming like a bat out of hell from the coast up north, a battlefield of the dead; wake up and smell the coffee, and the rotting in its wake. Still, every cloud has a silver lining. This is not of her doing, and yet it is also her hand at work. She used to crack walnuts in one trembling fist, strong as an ox, she was. She will cross the coast like an avenging angel at Cairns tomorrow morning or perhaps by lunchtime, proving there is no such thing as a free lunch.~~
~~I must put her in the ground before she wreaks havoc, warms the globe, raises tide-lines and steals whole continents out of the frying pan and into the fire.~~
~~There is a raised red patch of skin on my otherwise flawless, bronzed neck. I showered clean as a whistle when I arrived here. I put her ashes to ashes, dust to dust down on the bed and stepped under the crusted shower rose and bathed my body in the harsh water knowing what would happen if I did.~~
~~'Did we bring.. .... stuff?' I say.~~
~~'What allergy ....?' He says.~~
~~'You .... the ....?'~~
~~I can hear my other half searching in the overnight bag, the crinkle of a blister pack.~~
~~'...............?'~~
~~'No.'~~
~~'What's .... called?'~~
~~'Fexo-s................?It will say anti-histamine .... somewhere.'~~
~~The soft wamp of clothes falling to the carpet.~~
~~'No. ....could go to the chemist.'~~
~~'..............~~
~~.. Or~~
~~there is,~~
~~but an~~
~~hour~~
~~away.'~~
~~I scratch my back (and you scratch yours) and my nails leave fine red lines.~~
~~'...................?'~~
~~I give a wink and a nod. He couldn't see, but I hear some music, voices. He is glued to his phone.~~

~~***Category Four Cyclone***~~

~~*Large areas of the text are flattened.*~~
~~*Irreparable damage to paragraph structure.*~~
~~*Sentences are carried a considerable distance.*~~
~~*Extensive structural damage to the story*~~

~~The lid of the plastic vessel has a circle in the~~
~~top. The woman who handed it to me at~~
~~————————~~
~~———— the funeral place told me to pop it off with a knife.~~
~~There is no knife. I push at it with the~~

~~Cyclone Dragitsa by Cate Kennedy~~

There is a cyclone coming like a bat out of hell from the coast up north, a battlefield left in its wake.

Outside the rain starts up. On the long ride up here we were racing into it. Dark clouds, distant, then closer. Driving back down to Miriam Vale from the funeral place in Gladstone the clouds had begun to chase us.

'That's that cyclone,' my husband said, 'or the beginning of it.'

'Cyclone Dragitsa' I said, invoking her name, and he laughed, nodding in agreement.

I must put her in the ground before she wreaks havoc.

The tap will not stop dripping and the enamel is discoloured, light green, a deeper blue at the centre of the stain. A scab of salt on the scrubbed white of the bowl.

I showered when I arrived here at the motel. I put her ashes down on the ceramic sink and stepped under the crusted shower rose and bathed my body in the harsh bore water knowing what would happen if I did.

As a child I would wash myself in a bucket of rainwater drawn from the tank. In winter I would shiver between handfuls of warmth from water that was heated on the stove but always cooled too quickly. My hair was lank and limp with residual soap. I was jealous of my sister, my mother, my grandmother – all of them stepping lightly from a shower, pinked with the heat of it, clean and sweet with suds. But my skin would rebel against the hard groundwater; my arms flushing red, my chest flaring, itching. Naked and weeping in my bedroom I would dab at the spots with calamine lotion, replacing the red patches with splotches of white.

There was never a mirror in our house – which was lucky because I might have been turned to stone by the sight of my own skin – and my grandmother never allowed them. She would never approve of all these mirrors crammed into one tiny motel room; the full-length one in the bedroom, the one on the inside of the cupboard door.

And this one above the sink, throwing my own face back at me, sheened with sweat. I look damp and overblown. There is a raised red patch of skin on my neck.

'Did we bring any skin allergy stuff?' I call to my husband.

'What's it called?'

'In a blister pack. It'll say antihistamine somewhere.'

I hear him searching; clothes falling to the carpet.

'No, but I could go to the chemist.'

'There's no chemist. Or there is, but an hour away.'

I scratch my back and my nails leave fine red lines.

He is glued to his phone. I can hear him talking.

I lift my grandmother from the sink, and shake her. She sounds like a tub of sand. They have clothed her in a red velveteen bag with a gold pull cord, as if this is theatre. I imagine her climbing out of the container, pulling the cord like a magician. Reassembling herself in a puff of smoke. I long for and fear this in equal measure.

I can hear two people talking in the next room. A voice raised, a woman's voice. Then softer, a man. They are having an argument. I stop and listen but it is just the drone of voices like two bees trapped in a bottle. The lid of the container has a circle in the top. The woman who handed it to me at the funeral place told me to pop it off with a knife. There is no knife. I push at it with the rounded end of a teaspoon.

The rain comes, sudden and hard. It drowns out the argument next door despite its escalation. I wish they would stop. Whatever petty little detail caused their fury, nothing matters because I am holding her in my hands and she is both too heavy and too light and I am certain that now, at the death-end of things, she will come back to take us all out with her.

I turn the spoon around. The seal pops. I prise, and it comes off entirely.

I look inside and it isn't sand, it is coarser, and a strange pinking grey in colour. A chemical, synthetic reek.

There is nothing of my grandmother in here.

Still, I pour a small measure into a plastic vial.

I dip my finger in, touch it, pick a pinch up between my thumb and forefinger.

I place it on my tongue. I swallow.

Stones. Bones.

She used to crack walnuts in one trembling fist, strong as an ox.

The wind picks up, howls. The corrugated awning outside the motel room rattles violently. The people arguing next door are silenced by the sound of it. We are all a hush.

'Are you ok in there?'

The sound of my husband's voice.

I give a nod he can't see.

'That storm's going to be a beauty,' he calls.

I have to get her in the ground.

Cyclone Dragitsa

~~There is a~~The cyclone swarms, like a crocodile coming ~~like a bat out of hell~~ in from the ~~coast up~~ north~~, a battlefield left in~~. It snaps and flicks its ~~wake.~~ tail, moving slowly but with force and vigour and anger. How can you shake that which you carry so close?

Outside the rain ~~starts up~~strengthens.

On the ~~long~~ ride up here we were racing into it~~,~~. now we hunker down. Dark clouds, distant~~,~~; then closer. Driving back down to Miriam Vale from the funeral place in Gladstone the clouds had begun to chase us.

'That's that cyclone,' my husband said~~,~~ ~~'or~~. 'Or the beginning of it.'

'Cyclone Dragitsa' I said, invoking her name, and he laughed~~, nodding in agreement~~.

I must put her in the ground before she wreaks havoc.

The tap will not stop dripping ~~and the~~. The enamel is discoloured, light green, a deeper blue at the centre of the stain. A scab of salt on the scrubbed white of the bowl.

I showered when I arrived here at the motel. I put her ashes ~~down~~ on the ceramic sink and stepped under the crusted shower rose and bathed my body in the harsh bore water knowing what would happen if I did.

As a child I would wash myself in ~~a bucket of~~ rainwater drawn from the tank. In winter I would shiver ~~between handfuls of warmth from~~with water that was heated on the stove, but always cooled too quickly. My hair was lank and limp with residual soap. I was jealous of my sister, my mother, my grandmother—all of them stepping lightly from a shower, pinked with the heat of it, clean and sweet with suds. But my skin would rebel against the hard groundwater; my arms flushing red, my chest flaring, itching. Naked and weeping in my bedroom I would dab at the spots with calamine lotion, replacing the red patches with splotches of white.

There was never a mirror in our house—~~—~~which was lucky because I might have been turned to stone by the sight of my own skin~~—~~—and my grandmother never allowed them. She would never approve of all these mirrors crammed into one tiny motel room; the full-length one in the bedroom, the one on the inside of the cupboard door. Nothing to see inside here but ourselves.

And this one above the sink, throwing my ~~own~~ face back at me, sheened with sweat. I look damp and overblown. There is a raised red patch of skin on my neck.

'Did we bring any skin allergy stuff?' I call to my husband.

'What's it called?'

'In a blister pack. It'll say antihistamine somewhere.'

~~I hear him searching~~He searches; clothes falling to the carpet.

'No, but I could go to the chemist.'

'There's no chemist. ~~Or there is, but~~Well, an hour away.'

I scratch my back and my nails leave fine red lines.

He is glued to his phone. I can hear him talking.

I lift my grandmother from the sink, and shake ~~her~~. She sounds like a ~~tub~~million pieces of ~~sand~~nothing. They have clothed her in a red velveteen bag with a gold pull cord, as if this is theatre. I imagine her climbing out of the container, pulling the cord like a magician. Reassembling herself in a puff of smoke. I long for and fear this ~~in equal measure~~.

I can hear two people talking in the next room. A voice raised, a woman's voice. Then~~-~~—softer~~,~~ in comparison, but still loud as the cyclone closes on us—a man. ~~They are having an argument~~Arguing. I stop and listen but it is just the drone of voices like two bees trapped in a bottle. The lid of the container has a circle in the top. The woman who handed it to me at the funeral place told me to pop it off with a knife. There is no knife. I push at it with the rounded end of a teaspoon. The rain comes~~, sudden~~ harder and ~~hard. It~~ drowns out the argument next door despite its escalation. I wish they would stop. Whatever petty little detail caused their fury, nothing matters because I am holding her in my hands and she is ~~both~~ too heavy and too light and I am certain that now, at the death-end of things, she will come back to take us all out with her. I wonder if I could wipe my grandmother across me, like a salve and turn my skin into hers. I could bathe and exfoliate my skin with her.

I turn the spoon around. The seal pops. I prise, and it comes off entirely.

I look inside and it isn't sand, it is
coarser, and a strange pinking grey ~~in colour~~. A chemical, synthetic reek.
There is nothing of my grandmother in
here.
Still, I pour a small measure into a plastic
vial.
I dip my finger in, touch it, pick a pinch
up between my thumb and forefinger.
I place it on my tongue. I swallow. If not
outside, then in.
Stones. Bones.
She used to crack walnuts in one
trembling fist, strong as an ox.

The wind picks up, howls. The
corrugated awning outside the motel
room rattles violently. The people
arguing next door are silenced by the
sound of it. We are all a hush.
'Are you OK in there?'
The sound of my husband's voice.
I give a nod he can't see.
'That storm's going to be a beauty,' he
calls.
I have to get her in the ground.

Cyclone Dragitsa by Robert Hoge

The cyclone swarms, like a crocodile coming in from the north. It snaps and flicks its tail, moving slowly but with force and vigour and anger. How can you shake that which you carry so close?

Outside the rain strengthens. On the ride up here we were racing into it, now we hunker down. Dark clouds, distant; then closer. Driving back down to Miriam Vale from the funeral place in Gladstone the clouds had begun to chase us.

'That's that cyclone,' my husband said. 'Or the beginning of it.'

'Cyclone Dragitsa' I said, invoking her name, and he laughed.

I must put her in the ground before she wreaks havoc.

The tap will not stop dripping. The enamel is discoloured, light green, a deeper blue at the centre of the stain. A scab of salt on the scrubbed white of the bowl.

I showered when I arrived here at the motel. I put her ashes on the ceramic sink and stepped under the crusted shower rose and bathed my body in the harsh bore water knowing what would happen if I did.

As a child I would wash myself in rainwater drawn from the tank. In winter I would shiver with water that was heated on the stove, but always cooled too quickly. My hair was lank and limp with residual soap. I was jealous of my sister, my mother, my grandmother – all of them stepping lightly from a shower, pinked with the heat of it, clean and sweet with suds. But my skin would rebel against the hard groundwater; my arms flushing red, my chest flaring, itching. Naked and weeping in my bedroom I would dab at the spots with calamine lotion, replacing the red patches with splotches of white.

There was never a mirror in our house – which was lucky because I might have been turned to stone by the sight of my own skin – and my grandmother never allowed them. She would never approve of all these mirrors crammed into one tiny motel room; the full-length one in the bedroom, the one on the inside of the cupboard door. Nothing to see inside here but ourselves.

And this one above the sink, throwing my face back at me, sheened with sweat. I look damp and overblown. There is a raised red patch of skin on my neck.

'Did we bring any skin allergy stuff?' I call to my husband.

'What's it called?'

'In a blister pack. It'll say antihistamine somewhere.'

He searches; clothes falling to the carpet.

'No, but I could go to the chemist.'

'There's no chemist. Well, an hour away.'

I scratch my back and my nails leave fine red lines.

He is glued to his phone. I can hear him talking.

I lift my grandmother from the sink, and shake. She sounds like a million pieces of nothing. They have clothed her in a red velveteen bag with a gold pull cord, as if this is theatre. I imagine her climbing out of the container, pulling the cord like a magician. Reassembling herself in a puff of smoke. I long for and fear this.

I can hear two people talking in the next room. A voice raised, a woman's voice. Then – softer in comparison, but still loud as the cyclone closes on us – a man. Arguing. I stop and listen but it is just the drone of voices like two bees trapped in a bottle. The lid of the container has a circle in the top. The woman who handed it to me at the funeral place told me to pop it off with a knife. There is no knife. I push at it with the rounded end of a teaspoon.

The rain comes harder and drowns out the argument next door despite its escalation. I wish they would stop. Whatever petty little detail caused their fury, nothing matters because I am holding her in my hands and she is too heavy and too light and I am certain that now, at the death-end of things, she will come back to take us all out with her. I wonder if I could wipe my grandmother across me, like a salve and turn my skin into hers. I could bathe and exfoliate my skin with her.

I turn the spoon around. The seal pops. I prise, and it comes off entirely.

I look inside and it isn't sand, it is coarser, and a strange pinking grey. A chemical, synthetic reek.

There is nothing of my grandmother in here.

Still, I pour a small measure into a plastic vial.

I dip my finger in, touch it, pick a pinch up between my thumb and forefinger.

I place it on my tongue. I swallow. If not outside, then in.

Stones. Bones.

She used to crack walnuts in one trembling fist, strong as an ox.

The wind picks up, howls. The corrugated awning outside the motel room rattles violently. The people arguing next door are silenced by the sound of it. We are all a hush.

'Are you ok in there?'

The sound of my husband's voice.

I give a nod he can't see.

'That storm's going to be a beauty,' he calls.

I have to get her in the ground.

Cyclone ~~Dragitsa~~Dragista

~~The cyclone swarms, like a crocodile coming in from the north. It snaps and flicks its tail, moving slowly but with force and vigour and anger. How can you shake that which you carry so close? Outside the rain strengthens. On the ride up here we were racing into it, now we hunker down. Dark clouds, distant, then closer. Driving back down to Miriam Vale from the funeral place in Gladstone the clouds had begun to chase us.~~

~~'That's that cyclone,' my husband said. 'Or the beginning of it.'~~

~~'Cyclone Dragitsa' I said, invoking her name, and he laughed.~~

~~I must put her in the ground before she wreaks havoc.~~

~~The tap will not stop dripping. The enamel is discoloured, light green, a deeper blue at the centre of the stain. A scab of salt on the scrubbed white of the bowl.~~

~~I showered when I arrived here at the motel. I put her ashes on the ceramic sink and stepped under the crusted shower rose and bathed my body in the harsh bore water knowing what would happen if I did.~~

~~As a child I would wash myself in rainwater drawn from the tank. In winter I would shiver with water that was heated on the stove, but always cooled too quickly. My hair was lank and limp with residual soap. I was jealous of my sister, my mother, my grandmother—all of them stepping lightly from a shower, pinked with the heat of it, clean and sweet with suds. But my skin would rebel against the hard groundwater, my arms flushing red, my chest flaring, itching. Naked and weeping in my bedroom I would dab at the spots with calamine lotion, replacing the red patches with splotches of white.~~

~~There was never a mirror in our house – which was lucky because I might have been turned to stone by the sight of my own skin – and my grandmother never allowed them. She would never approve of all these mirrors crammed into one tiny motel room, the full-length one in the bedroom, the one on the inside of the cupboard door. Nothing to see inside here but ourselves.~~

~~And this one above the sink, throwing my face back at me, sheened with sweat. I look damp and overblown. There is a raised red patch of skin on my neck.~~

~~'Did we bring any skin allergy stuff?' I call to my husband.~~

~~'What's it called?'~~

~~'In a blister pack. It'll say antihistamine somewhere.'~~

~~He searches, clothes falling to the carpet.~~

~~'No, but I could go to the chemist.'~~

~~'There's no chemist. Well, an hour away.'~~

~~I scratch my back and my nails leave fine red lines.~~

~~He is glued to his phone. I can hear him talking.~~

~~I lift my grandmother from the sink, and shake. She sounds like a million pieces of nothing. They have clothed her in a red velveteen bag with a gold pull cord, as if this is theatre. I imagine her climbing out of the container, pulling the cord like a magician. Reassembling herself in a puff of smoke. I long for and fear this.~~

~~I can hear two people talking in the next room. A voice raised, a woman's voice. Then – softer in comparison, but still loud as the cyclone closes on us – a man. Arguing. I stop and listen but it is just the drone of voices like two bees trapped in a bottle. The lid of the container has a circle in the top. The woman who handed it to me at the funeral place told me to pop it off with a knife. There is no knife. I push at it with the rounded end of a teaspoon.~~

~~The rain comes harder and drowns out the argument next door despite its escalation. I wish they would stop. Whatever petty little detail caused their fury, nothing matters because I am holding her in my hands and she is too heavy and too light and I am certain that now, at the death-end of things, she will come back to take us all out with her. I wonder if I could wipe my grandmother across me, like a salve and turn my skin into hers. I could bathe and exfoliate my skin with her.~~

~~I turn the spoon around. The seal pops. I prise, and it comes off entirely.~~

~~I look inside and it isn't sand, it is coarser, and a strange pinking grey. A chemical, synthetic reek.~~

~~There is nothing of my grandmother in here.~~

~~Still, I pour a small measure into a plastic vial.~~

~~I dip my finger in, touch it, pick a pinch up between my thumb and forefinger.~~

~~I place it on my tongue. I swallow. If not outside, then in.~~
~~Stones. Bones.~~
~~She used to crack walnuts in one trembling fist, strong as an ox.~~

~~The wind picks up, howls. The corrugated awning outside the motel room rattles violently. The people arguing next door are silenced by the sound of it. We are all a hush.~~
~~'Are you OK in there?'~~
~~The sound of my husband's voice.~~
~~I give a nod he can't see.~~
~~'That storm's going to be a beauty,' he calls.~~
~~I have to get her in the ground.~~
In my eye there is a deep calm, a great stillness untouched by the mayhem that swirls around me, and it was during this lull as my eye passed over the land and the silence fell that the woman came out of the squat brick hotel which had hugged the ground during the worst of the storm as palm trees bent down before me and houses disassembled themselves and sheets of corrugated iron sliced the air and driverless cars slid heedlessly along the roads while my front passed over the town.

Now, in the exhausted pause, water sluiced the muddy ground and there was not a foothold anywhere and the woman slipped and fell on her side but she did not make a sound or let go of the jar she clutched to her as if it was a child, and when she stood up half her body was dripping brown muck and her hair hung in ropes and she looked around, surveying the flattened landscape – the rows of roofless shells and twisted girders, the felled powerlines, the plastic outdoor tables and chairs floating down the street, the ghostly supermarket bags flapping from broken branches, the fields of prone sugar cane and in the distance, the grey waves clawing the sea wall – and with eyes that had seen too much, she settled on a spot beneath a tree of unrecognisable genus that had been ripped from the ground at the roots.

With careful, determined steps, she moved towards the horizontal trunk with its exposed roots clenched in a gnarled fist and when she reached the hole in the ground that had once housed these roots, a hole filled with water as black as outer space, she dropped to her knees and placed the jar at her side and began to bail the water with her bare hands until nothing but oily sludge remained at the bottom and into this primeval slime she thrust the jar, dragging mud from all around to bury it, and then she slowly got to her feet and said, 'Now leave us be'.

All my life I have been spinning in circles, with no beginning and no end, and when I look backward I see only chaos and destruction and hear only the howls of rage and fear of those who are no longer, their disembodied voices rising like a choir of the dead, and when I look forward I see the same, and yet at my core all is hushed and tranquil and unmoved as birds scatter before me and animals dive into burrows in which they will drown and humans fleeing in cars are sent skidding towards infinity, and I watch with my eye that sees all and understands nothing.

As the woman stared down on the grave she had made for the jar, a man staggered out from the hotel which was the only building still standing for miles around, and slipping and sliding across the mud he cursed and yelled at her to come back inside because the danger was not yet over, the blue skies meant nothing, there was more violence to come, and when he reached her, his face was contorted and his mouth misshapen and he asked her what she thought was doing and she looked at him with eyes as calm and clear as my own, telling him she had to do it, had get the ashes into the ground because all this devastation was her grandmother's doing and that only when her ashes were returned to the earth would everything would be all right.

The man grabbed at his hair and gripped it as if to tear it out and told her that this was the madness of grief, that her grandmother was dead and gone, and that the cyclone was a creature of nature, born of tropical seas, of spiralling heat-laden waters transformed into furious squalls and pelting rains and towering waves, and that with the oceans growing steadily warmer over recent times their off-spring has increased in number and in deadly force, like spiderlings hatched by the heat, and as he spoke of my origins I knew that it was the truth and that I still carried this tropical sea in my clouds and

~~Cyclone Dragista by Fiona Capp~~

In my eye there is a deep calm, a great stillness untouched by the mayhem that swirls around me, and it was during this lull as my eye passed over the land and the silence fell that the woman came out of the squat brick hotel which had hugged the ground during the worst of the storm as palm trees bent down before me and houses disassembled themselves and sheets of corrugated iron sliced the air and driverless cars slid heedlessly along the roads while my front passed over the town.

Now, in the exhausted pause, water sluiced the muddy ground and there was not a foothold anywhere and the woman slipped and fell on her side but she did not make a sound or let go of the jar she clutched to her as if it was a child and, when she stood up, half her body was dripping brown muck and her hair hung in ropes and she looked around, surveying the flattened landscape – the rows of roofless shells and twisted girders, the felled powerlines, the plastic outdoor tables and chairs floating down the street, the ghostly supermarket bags flapping from broken branches, the fields of prone sugar cane and in the distance, the grey waves clawing the sea wall – and with eyes that had seen too much, she settled on a spot beneath a tree of unrecognisable genus that had been ripped from the ground at the roots.

With careful, determined steps, she moved towards the horizontal trunk with its exposed roots clenched in a gnarled fist and when she reached the hole in the ground that had once housed these roots, a hole filled with water as black as outer space, she dropped to her knees and placed the jar at her side and began to bail the water with her bare hands until nothing but oily sludge remained at the bottom and into this primeval slime she thrust the jar, dragging mud from all around to bury it, and then she slowly got to her feet and said, 'Now leave us be.'

All my life I have been spinning in circles, with no beginning and no end, and when I look backward I see only chaos and destruction and hear only the howls of rage and fear of those who are no longer, their disembodied voices rising like a choir of the dead, and when I look forward I see the same, and yet at my core all is hushed and tranquil and unmoved as birds scatter before me and animals dive into burrows in which they will drown and humans fleeing in cars are sent skidding towards infinity, and I watch with my eye that sees all and understands nothing.

As the woman stared down on the grave she had made for the jar, a man staggered out from the hotel which was the only building still standing for miles around, and slipping and sliding across the mud he cursed and yelled at her to come back inside because the danger was not yet over, the blue skies meant nothing, there was more violence to come, and when he reached her, his face was contorted and his mouth misshapen and he asked her what she thought was doing and she looked at him with eyes as calm and clear as my own, telling him she had to do it, had get the ashes into the ground because all this devastation was her grandmother's doing and that only when her ashes were returned to the earth would everything would be all right.

The man grabbed at his hair and gripped it as if to tear it out and told her that this was the madness of grief, that her grandmother was dead and gone, and that the cyclone was a creature of nature, born of tropical seas, of spiralling heat-laden waters transformed into furious squalls and pelting rains and towering waves, and that with the oceans growing steadily warmer over recent times their offspring has increased in number and in deadly force, like spiderlings hatched by the heat, and as he spoke of my origins I knew that it was the truth and that I still carried this tropical sea in my clouds and that when I was finally spent, all my waters would return to this sea like those ashes returned to the earth.

And in this moment, I understood what I had been unable to understand before, I saw it all – that I, too, would come to an end like the puny, scuttling creatures on the earth below me, that like all living things I had only one life, already half over, and that even as my winds began to stir once again, the lull ending and the second storm front approaching like the Second Coming, I was hastening to my ruin.

At first the rain was soft and salty, like human tears, and then as my tempest came rushing into the silence and the stillness, sweeping over the man and the woman who clung to each other as they ran, the rain fell like spears hurled from the clouds and the gale force winds flung them to the ground and held them there while the waves, whipped up by the wind, surged high over the breakwater and raced across the land, and fed by the cataract raging down from the sky, it swept them both away, and the only human thing left in it all was its power to destroy everything in its path, everything that it touched.

And as my eye moved on and left them to their fate, I saw the jar, now disinterred by the waters, bobbing on the surface of the roiling current like a bottle with a message from a time of terrible innocence and wilful blindness, of superstition and denial, of greed and joy, before the flood.

Walking the Walk by Robert Hoge

Most people learn to walk just once.

An unlucky few need to stumble through it a second time after a schism of the back or a grody snap of the ankle. Then there's the rest of us – the leaners, the lame, the legless – a tribe who needs to learn to walk every time we get a new pair of prosthetic legs.

New prosthetics can come with a whole range of changes – they might be a different shade of dark cream, they may be lighter, stronger, more reliable. Once I collected a new pair and discovered that instead of a crescent moon of rubber at the tip of the feet, they suddenly had toes. My sister was so excited, she stole my legs so she could paint the toenails a rich, dark purple. Didn't suit my skin tone at all.

Sometimes – the golden growing summers of my youth – my prosthetic legs would grow longer and all of a sudden I'd be 5cm taller. There wasn't much about my appearance that filled me with pride when I was a kid, but leaving school one afternoon the third shortest student in class and coming back the next day the third tallest was pretty damn special.

With new feet came new sensations, with a new artificial knee came new challenges and with longer legs came a whole new gait. Imagine getting out of bed one morning and you're 7cm taller and your knee is 3cm lower. I'd stand up after putting on the new legs and feel like I was Dannii Minogue in a Kylie Minogue music video. I'd stand up, sway, lean to one side to stop swaying, over-correct and fall over – the strangest of locomotions. Try again. This time reaching out for the wall to hold myself up. Eventually I'd master standing up but everything else felt different – my hips, my back, how far my hands were from the ground. Putting one foot in front of the other should be simple, right? It should be dependable, knowable. It should be something you could rely on.

It's not a small thing. It's not like just getting a new pair of shoes because you get new feet to go inside them too – feet that are firmer because they've never been used. Throw in a new ankle to join it all to a new shin and maybe a new knee as well. All of that newness works instantly, universally to remind you of that one simple fact – you don't have any legs.

If you had legs, you wouldn't feel like you were walking on a foreign planet. You wouldn't fall over putting them on the first morning you had them because you hadn't 'walked in' the new set yet. The most disconcerting – legal – out-of-body experience you can get.

Maybe you know something of the feeling, like when you drive a new car for the first time. You might have had the old car for three years, maybe five. You were used to its quirks, how the right blinker was just that little bit sticky; how there was that slight knock when the engine went from first gear to second. How there was that slight dint in the licence plate that you never bothered getting fixed. Then you get the new car. The seat is different. The engine purrs but it isn't the same. Every time you try to turn a blinker on you end up with windscreen wipers going instead.

So how do you do it? Sheer necessity helps, I suppose. You could really swap sets of legs I suppose – like an opening batsmen choosing the bat that best suits him for the day. But mostly there's no going back. Once you start down the track you need to keep going. An average person might take two-and-a-half million to three million steps a year. You can normally adapt to new legs in less than a week – maybe 25,000 steps or so. Switching sets of legs just means re-adapting again and again.

And there's kind of a loveliness about it which makes you always conscious of your connection with the physical world. Your brain pauses for a second and re-discovers the world for you. This is the first time you've got in a car with these legs, and it feels different. The first time you've walked downstairs. The first time you've chugged up a hill. The first time you've tried to run, hoping that maybe just this once you'd be able to run. But it reminds you for just a few days that you're not really connected to the Earth. You – the real you – is floating three feet above the ground. Your legs are your freedom and your burden – your Dannii and your Kylie.

Walking becomes so ingrained after a while that when you get a new pair of legs you really do need to learn how to walk again. And it wasn't like it was easy to do in the first place. Now you're older; maybe fatter and certainly more set in your ways. You've worked out – walked out – the kinks in your legs. You know it's easier to step onto the sidewalk with your right leg because that's your leg with the real knee – the one you have more control over.

So you do it. You stand up, you lean, you stumble and fall and feel like every single step is Armstrong on the moon. You feel this crazy ambivalence to these tools of torturous freedom. You haven't worn them in yet. They rub in all the wrong places. You lift your left foot too high and put your right leg down too hard. You shout for joy because the new legs are lighter and fit better – not right yet – but better. But you crave the comfort and sameness of your old legs like someone quitting smoking craves having a pencil to roll across their fingers.

So, how do you do it? What is the secret for getting through the task? Like mastering most things it ends up being pretty simple – just keep putting one stump in front of the other.

Walking the walk, 2045.

The brand managers told us we were lucky to have come across the article in the archive. It's not often, they said, that we – by which they meant we here at Pro-aesthetic™ - had access to primary source material like this. They were calling a meeting with the Imagineers and the CEOs and we'd get together over an actual table and dream up the direction of the new campaign.

"It's an piece of writing," Jonathon enthused as we made our way to the Senior Executive floor for the meeting, "full of simple statements of insight, written with actual first-hand experience. No sales agenda, no pitch."

The managers were right – this was rare. By the time Pro-aesthetic had started making headway, back in the 20s, its primary market was amputees who were victims of old 20th century ordinance – the unexploded landmines that peppered warzones across the planet. With global viable farmland shrinking so much after the millenium, people were forced to venture back onto those zones – across Africa and Asia mostly – and we always had a stream of candidates who were willing – desperate even – for new improved limbs to replace their old ones. We hadn't needed much market research. But it was the raging spike across the industrialised world in diabetes that really consolidated our market share. Unprecedented demand for prosthetics really put us on the map. They'd been boom years for a while there – new legs all round, patented Innovative NewSkin, a knee joint that won us an international prize. Now it seemed we were headed in a new direction.

Inside the boardroom Jared, our wunderkind CEO, welcomed us.

"These are exciting days," he said, as he often did. "Our history may have felt slow and methodical, but I think, as this article will show us, that it's only been one short generation since the inception of a brilliantly fast and inventive revolution of which we are the proud vanguards."

He brought an image of a page to the screen. Plain text. Just one candid sentence after another.

"*Most people learn to walk just once*~~.~~ ~~An unlucky few need to stumble through it a second time after a schism of the back or a grody snap of the ankle.~~," it began. "...*Then there's the rest of us – the leaners, the lame, the legless – a tribe who needs to ~~learn to~~ walk every time we get a new pair of prosthetic legs*~~.~~." Jared highlighted the word 'tribe' with a single touch, saying nothing.

"*New prosthetics can come with a whole range of changes – they might be a different shade of dark cream, they may be lighter, stronger, more reliable. Once I collected a new pair and discovered that instead of a crescent moon of rubber at the tip of the feet, they suddenly had toes*~~.~~ ~~My sister was so excited, she stole my legs so she could paint the toenails a rich, dark purple. Didn't suit my skin tone at all.~~," continued the article.

Jared raised his eyebrows and responded to our smiles. "This is what I mean," he said. "you can see we were at the very beginning of not only the technology, but also the conception of its marketing possibilities. The idea of toes being new, being novel. And you can see here how he jokes about his sister, painting the toenails. This would have been – let's see – just a few short years before the app came out for incorporating interactive tattoos and the self-tanning feature became standard. Then the SuperReal Prosthetic Pro, the gamechanger. Remember the single idea that was based on?"

"Imitating the compression marks caused by sock elastic on the shins," said Jonathon. Jared paused, looked at him. "Right," he said. "But not *imitating*, Jon. *Reproducing*." He turned back to the page and read a passage aloud:

"*Sometimes – the golden growing summers of my youth – my prosthetic legs would grow lengthen and all of a sudden I'd be 5cm taller. There wasn't much about my appearance that filled me with pride when I was a kid, but leaving school one afternoon the third shortest student in class and coming back the next day the third tallest was pretty damn special*~~.~~,"

~~With new feet came new sensations, with a new artificial knee came new challenges and with longer legs came a whole new gait. Imagine getting out of bed one morning and you're 7cm taller and your knee is 3cm lower. I'd stand up after putting on the new legs and feel like I was Dannii Minogue in a Kylie Minogue music video. I'd stand up, sway, lean to one side to stop swaying, over-correct and fall over – the strangest of~~

~~locomotions. Try again. This time reaching out for the wall to hold myself up. Eventually I'd master standing up but everything else felt different – my hips, my back, how far my hands were from the ground.~~ "Hear that?" said Jared dreamily. " 'Golden'. 'Pride'. 'Pretty damn special'. That's what we're after, friends. That overwhelming emotional surge. How to *harness* that surge? How to nurture a *craving* for it? "

"*Putting one foot in front of the other should be simple, right. It should be dependable, knowable. It should be something you could rely on*~~.~~.."

~~It's not a small thing. It's not like just getting a new pair of shoes because you get new feet to go inside them too – feet that are firmer because they've never been used. Throw in a new ankle to join it all to a new shin and maybe a new knee as well. All of that newness works instantly, universally to remind you of that one simple fact – you don't have any legs.~~

~~If you had legs, you wouldn't feel like you were walking on a foreign planet. You wouldn't fall over putting them on the first morning you had them because you hadn't 'walked in' the new set yet. The most disconcerting – legal – out-of-body experience you can get.~~

~~Maybe you know something of the feeling, like when you drive a new car for the first time. You might have had the old car for three years, maybe five. You were used to its quirks, how the right blinker was just that little bit sticky; how there was that slight knock when the engine went from first gear to second. How there was that slight dint in the licence plate that you never bothered getting fixed. Then you get the new car. The seat is different. The engine purrs but it isn't the same. Every time you try to turn a blinker on you end up with windscreen wipers going instead.~~

~~So how do you do it? Sheer necessity helps, I suppose.~~ "I know you've all read reports from diabetic amputees from the old days which echoed this fundamental frustration," said Jared. "They just wanted something reliable and straightforward, something that didn't draw attention to the fact that their legs were prosthetic. And that market's still bullish, don't you worry. Diabetes is our bread and butter, as it were. But our customers.. how can I put this. We love novelty, but we love normalising. We don't mind spending to make a statement. And more and more of our clients feel encouraged now to purchase multiple sets from Pro-aesthetic, because they can see, as we can, that the sky's the limit and it's discriminatory to restrict options to consumer choice. Why not, after all, have a set for every day of the week, for each season, for every whim, if that's what you want? Why not develop Pro-aesthetic limbs which reproduce the appearance of gradually increasing muscle tone of the calves, or adjust skin tone according to mood? You can see it already, if you've got the eyes to see it - in an early article like this one, straight from the heart of a person without legs – the possibility there, germinating."

He pointed to another sentence: "*You could really swap sets of legs I suppose – like an opening batsmen choosing the bat that best suits him for the day*~~. But mostly there's no going back. Once you start down the track you need to keep going. An average person might take two-and-a-half million to three million steps a year. You can normally adapt to new legs in less than a week – maybe 25,000 steps or so.~~ ...*Switching sets of legs just means re-adapting again and again*~~.~~.."

"Thirty years ago," said Jared, musing. "Re-adapting again and again.. .there's something in there for all of us to reflect on."

"The biggest sales spike last year," added the other wunderkind, Mark from Brand Mapping, "was Carefree Barefoot™, right? Because that just needed a conceptual leap. Why wear shoes, if you're wearing prosthetic legs? Why not just make the synthetic soles indestructible?"

"Thanks for bringing that up, Skye," answered Jared. "Because that kind of segues in a neat way into what I want to touch on next. That indicates a shift, the Carefree Barefoot™. A sign of a falling away of stigma, of a desire to be proud. A statement that says, "hey – I'm not hiding anything! I'm wearing these legs because I'm making a consumer choice to do so!"

He paused to let this sink in. "So what's the way forward now?" he said softly.

Walking the Walk, 2045 by Cate Kennedy

The brand managers told us we were lucky to have come across the article in the archive. It's not often, they said, that we – by which they meant we here at Pro-aesthetic™ – had access to primary source material like this. They were calling a meeting with the Imagineers and the CEOs and we'd get together over an actual table and dream up the direction of the new campaign.

'It's a piece of writing,' Jonathon enthused as we made our way to the Senior Executive floor for the meeting, 'full of simple statements of insight, written with actual first-hand experience. No sales agenda, no pitch.'

The managers were right – this was rare. By the time Pro-aesthetic had started making headway, back in the 20s, its primary market was amputees who were victims of old 20th century ordinance – the unexploded landmines that peppered warzones across the planet. With global viable farmland shrinking so much after the millenium, people were forced to venture back onto those zones – across Africa and Asia mostly – and we always had a stream of candidates who were willing – desperate even – for new improved limbs to replace their old ones. We hadn't needed much market research. But it was the raging spike across the industrialised world in diabetes that really consolidated our market share. Unprecedented demand for prosthetics really put us on the map.

They'd been boom years for a while there – new legs all round, patented Innovative NewSkin, a knee joint that won us an international prize. Now it seemed we were headed in a new direction.

Inside the boardroom Jared, our wunderkind CEO, welcomed us.

'These are exciting days,' he said, as he often did. 'Our history may have felt slow and methodical, but I think, as this article will show us, that it's only been one short generation since the inception of a brilliantly fast and inventive revolution of which we are the proud vanguards.'

He brought an image of a page to the screen. Plain text. Just one candid sentence after another.

'Most people learn to walk just once.' it began. '…Then there's the rest of us – the leaners, the lame, the legless – a tribe who needs to walk every time we get a new pair of prosthetic legs.' Jared highlighted the word 'tribe' with a single touch, saying nothing.

'New prosthetics can come with a whole range of changes – they might be a different shade of dark cream, they may be lighter, stronger, more reliable. Once I collected a new pair and discovered that instead of a crescent moon of rubber at the tip of the feet, they suddenly had toes.' continued the article.

Jared raised his eyebrows and responded to our smiles. 'This is what I mean,' he said. 'you can see we were at the very beginning of not only the technology, but also the conception of its marketing possibilities. The idea of toes being new, being novel. And you can see here how he jokes about his sister, painting the toenails. This would have been – let's see – just a few short years before the app came out for incorporating interactive tattoos and the self-tanning feature became standard. Then the SuperReal Prosthetic Pro, the gamechanger. Remember the single idea that was based on?'

'Imitating the compression marks caused by sock elastic on the shins,' said Jonathon. Jared paused, looked at him.

'Right,' he said. 'But not imitating, Jon. Reproducing.' He turned back to the page and read a passage aloud:

'"Sometimes – the golden growing summers of my youth – my prosthetic legs would grow lengthen and all of a sudden I'd be 5cm taller. There wasn't much about my appearance that filled me with pride when I was a kid, but leaving school one afternoon the third shortest student in class and coming back the next day the third tallest was pretty damn special."

'Hear that?' said Jared dreamily. '"Golden". "Pride". "Pretty damn special". That's what we're after, friends. That overwhelming emotional surge. How to harness that surge? How to nurture a craving for it?

'Putting one foot in front of the other should be simple, right. It should be dependable, knowable. It should be something you could rely on.

'I know you've all read reports from diabetic amputees from the old days which echoed this fundamental frustration,' said Jared. 'They just wanted something reliable and straightforward, something that didn't draw attention to the fact that their legs were prosthetic. And that market's still bullish, don't you worry. Diabetes is our bread and butter, as it were. But our customers…how can I put this. We love novelty, but we love normalising. We don't mind spending to make a statement. And more and more of our clients feel encouraged now to purchase multiple sets from Pro-aesthetic, because they can see, as we can, that the sky's the limit and it's discriminatory to restrict options to consumer choice. Why not, after all, have a set for every day of the week, for each season, for every whim, if that's what you want? Why not develop Pro-aesthetic limbs which reproduce the appearance of gradually increasing muscle tone of the calves, or adjust skin tone according to mood? You can see it already, if you've got the eyes to see it – in an early article like this one, straight from the heart of a person without legs – the possibility there, germinating.'

He pointed to another sentence: '"You could really swap sets of legs I suppose – like an opening batsmen choosing the bat that best suits him for the day …Switching sets of legs just means re-adapting again and again."'

'Thirty years ago,' said Jared, musing. '"Re-adapting again and again"….there's something in there for all of us to reflect on.'

'The biggest sales spike last year,' added the other wunderkind, Skye from Brand Mapping, 'was Carefree Barefoot™, right? Because that just needed a conceptual leap. Why wear shoes, if you're wearing prosthetic legs? Why not just make the synthetic soles indestructible?'

'Thanks for bringing that up, Skye,' answered Jared. 'Because that kind of segues in a neat way into what I want to touch on next. That indicates a shift, the Carefree Barefoot™. A sign of a falling away of stigma, of a desire to be proud. A statement that says, 'hey – I'm not hiding anything! I'm wearing these legs because I'm making a consumer choice to do so!'

He paused to let this sink in. 'So what's the way forward now?' he said softly. 'Where's the path? How can we capitalise on this shift? It's in this piece of writing, in my opinion; this simple sincere piece written three decades ago. Just let's...look.'

He raised his finger and highlighted another fragment of text.

'"And there's kind of a loveliness about it which makes you always conscious of your connection with the physical world. Your brain pauses for a second and re-discovers the world for you. This is the first time you've got in a car with these legs, and it feels different. The first time you've walked downstairs. The first time you've chugged up a hill. The first time you've tried to run, hoping that maybe just this once you'd be able to run. But it reminds you for just a few days that you're not really connected to the Earth. You – the real you – is floating three feet above the ground. Your legs are your freedom and your burden."

'"Your freedom and your burden",' said Jared in the same dreamy voice. 'There's a keystone slogan for us right there. "The real you." And don't you love that? "...a kind of loveliness which makes you conscious of your connection with the physical world." That's what we need to think about now. Something elemental and visceral – something that does nothing less than re-discover the world for you.'

He turned back to us and spread his arms in entreaty. 'So my challenge to you today is – do we have it in us to be audacious? Where is our new market? Where is our new fertile ground?'

'Are you talking increased vertical market saturation?' said Skye.

Jared eyed him patiently. 'I'm talking "golden". I'm talking "pride". I'm talking "pretty damn special". There's limited prestige in contracting Type 2 Diabetes, Skye. We can recover that prestige with fabulous product, sure, we can restore the sense of choice and control to turn that around, but what if we take that – if you'll forgive me – a step further? What if we began to create customised, state-of-the-art Proaesthetic improved limb enhancement options for a more discerning client? A client not afraid to take the steps to be pretty damn special?'

He stared at us, and we stared back. A glimmering of understanding of what he was saying. This was the genius of Jared, I couldn't help thinking in that silence. Seeing this in context. What begins as tattooing and morphs into body piercing and scarification and plastic surgery and then anything for novelty, anything to embellish, to strut, to revise, to reinvent.

'You're talking…voluntary amputation,' said Skye hesitantly.

'Stop,' Jared said sharply. 'I don't want to hear the "a" word. I never want to hear it again in any of our promotional copy, is that understood? I don't even like "voluntary". And definitely not "cutting edge", for obvious reasons.'

A nervous ripple of uncertain laughter greeted this.

'I like "elective",' went on Jared. 'I like "pro-active". I like to think of this as "pro-active cosmetic enhancement".' He looked sternly across the room, full of faces gazing back at him. 'Language is everything,' he said. 'We've got to make choosing to incorporate enhanced and eternally youthful limbs the ultimate statement. Of fashion. Of art. Of primal attraction. Remember that word – tribe. That's our touchstone. I know we can do it.'

Brainstorm time, because even now, in the middle of the 21st century, groups of image marketeers still swear by brainstorming. We cleared our throats and shifted in our seats. Cast covert, anxious glances at each other. Secretly, everyone was wondering what I was nervously wondering, I suspect – what would our real test be, as our company's executive team, to publicly demonstrate brand loyalty? What would be asked of us? What is the secret for getting through the task of taking this next impossible step?

Walking the ~~walk, 2045~~ Walk. 2050

~~The brand managers told us we were lucky to have come across the article in the archive. It's not often, they said, that we—by which they meant we here at Pro-aesthetic™—had access to primary source material like this. They were calling a meeting with the Imagineers and the CEOs and we'd get together over an actual table and dream up the direction of the new campaign.~~

~~'It's an piece of writing,' Jonathon enthused as we made our way to the Senior Executive floor for the meeting, 'full of simple statements of insight, written with actual first-hand experience. No sales agenda, no pitch.'~~

~~The managers were right—this was rare. By the time Pro-aesthetic had started making headway, back~~When Christopher got the job with Pro-aesthetic as an imagineer he was over moon and so was I. He had spent two, dispiriting years searching for work after graduating in Imagineering – in my day we called it marketing – and copping knock back after knock back. A few times, he reached the second round of interviews, but that was as far as it went. I had started to worry that he was too good for the world and would never get the break he deserved.

At school, his teachers often described him as 'impressionable' and 'easily lead' which meant that he occasionally got into strife. But he was a sweet natured boy and they could see this. He desperately wanted to be popular, to be with the in-group, which made him somewhat slavish in his attention to fashion and the latest trends. In job interviews, he was always trying to say the right thing and I suspect that he came across as a little too eager to please. At school, the nastier kids used to call him a suck.

If only he were only given the chance to prove himself, I was sure he would shine. But now, when I look back on what happened, I can't help feeling that Pro-aesthetic chose him precisely because they saw him as pliable, an employee who would sacrifice his best interests for the sake of holding on to his job; a perfect mannequin for the company.

When Christopher started at Pro-aesthetic, the company was best known for consolidating its market share in prosthetics for diabetics, which was ravaging the Industrialised world. Back in the 20s, its primary market was amputees who were victims of old 20th century ordinance—the ~~unexploded~~ landmines that peppered warzones across the planet. With global viable farmland shrinking so much after the ~~milenium~~millennium, people were forced to venture back onto those zones ~~–~~—across Africa and Asia mostly~~–~~— and ~~we always~~the company had a stream of candidates who were ~~willing –~~will, desperate even~~–~~, for new improved limbs to replace their old ones. ~~We hadn't needed much market research. But it was the raging spike across the industrialised world in diabetes that really consolidated our market share. Unprecedented demand for prosthetics really put us on the map.~~

~~They'd been boom years for a while there—new legs all round, patented Innovative~~ Before applying for the job, Christopher did his homework on the company's biggest innovations— NewSkin, a knee joint that won ~~us~~them an international prize~~. Now it seemed we were headed in a new direction.~~

~~Inside the boardroom Jared, our wunderkind CEO, welcomed us.~~

~~'These are exciting days,' he said, as he often did. 'Our history may have felt slow and methodical, but I think, as this article will show us, that it's only been one short generation since the inception of a brilliantly fast and inventive revolution of which we are the proud vanguards.'~~

~~He brought an image of a page to the screen. Plain text. Just one candid sentence after another.~~

~~'*Most people learn to walk just once.*' it began. '*... Then there's the rest of us – the leaners, the lame, the legless – a tribe who needs to walk every time we get a new pair of prosthetic legs.*' Jared highlighted the word 'tribe' with a single touch, saying nothing.~~

~~'*New prosthetics can come with a whole range of changes – they might be a different shade of dark cream, they may be lighter, stronger, more reliable. Once I collected a new pair and discovered that instead of a crescent moon of rubber at the tip of the feet, they suddenly had toes.*' continued the article.~~

~~Jared raised his eyebrows and responded to our smiles. 'This is what I mean,' he said. 'you can see we were at the very beginning of not only the technology, but also the conception of its marketing possibilities. The idea of~~

~~toes being new, being novel. And you can see here how he jokes about his sister, painting the toenails. This would have been – let's see – just a few short years before the app came out for incorporating interactive tattoos and the self-tanning feature became standard. Then the~~, Carefree Barefoot with indestructible synthetic soles and SuperReal Prosthetic Pro, the gamechanger~~. Remember the single idea that was based on?'~~

~~'Imitating the compression~~ which was so lifelike and responsive it could reproduce the marks caused by sock elastic ~~on the shins,' said Jonathon. Jared paused, looked at him.~~

~~'Right,' he said. 'But not *imitating*, Jon. *Reproducing*.' He turned back to the page and read a passage aloud:~~

~~*'Sometimes – the golden growing summers of my youth – my prosthetic legs would grow lengthen and all of a sudden I'd be 5cm taller. There wasn't much about my appearance that filled me with pride when I was a kid, but leaving school one afternoon the third shortest student in class and coming back the next day the third tallest was pretty damn special.'*~~

~~'Hear that?' said Jared dreamily. '"Golden". "Pride". "Pretty damn special". That's what we're after, friends. That overwhelming emotional surge. How to *harness* that surge? How to nurture a *craving* for it?'~~

~~*'Putting one foot in front of the other should be simple, right. It should be dependable, knowable. It should be something you could rely on.'*~~

~~'I know you've all read reports from diabetic amputees from the old days which echoed this fundamental frustration,' said Jared. 'They just wanted something reliable and straightforward, something that didn't draw attention to the fact that their legs were prosthetic. And that market's still bullish, don't you worry. Diabetes is our bread and butter, as it were. But our customers.. how can I put this. We love novelty, but we love normalising. We don't mind spending to make a statement. And more and more of our clients feel encouraged now to purchase multiple sets from Pro-aesthetic, because they can see, as we can, that the sky's the limit and it's discriminatory to restrict options to consumer choice. Why not, after all, have a set for every day of the week, for each season, for every whim, if that's what you want? Why not develop Pro-aesthetic limbs which reproduce the appearance of gradually increasing muscle tone of the calves, or adjust skin tone according to mood? You can see it already, if you've got the eyes to see it – in an early article like this one, straight from the heart of a person without legs – the possibility there, germinating.'~~

~~He pointed to another sentence: *'You could really swap sets of legs I suppose – like an opening batsmen choosing the bat that best suits him for the day... Switching sets of legs just means re-adapting again and again..'*~~

~~'Thirty years ago,' said Jared, musing. 'Re-adapting again and again... there's something in there for all of us to reflect on.'~~

~~'The biggest sales spike last year,' added the other wunderkind, Mark from Brand Mapping, 'was Carefree Barefoot™, right? Because that just needed a conceptual leap. Why wear shoes, if you're wearing prosthetic legs? Why not just make the synthetic soles indestructible?'~~

~~'Thanks for bringing that up, Skye,' answered Jared. 'Because that kind of segues in a neat way into what I want to touch on next. That indicates a shift, the Carefree Barefoot™. A sign of a falling away of stigma, of a desire to be proud. A statement that says, 'hey – I'm not hiding anything! I'm wearing these legs because I'm making a consumer choice to do so!'~~

~~He paused to let this sink in. 'So what's the way forward now?' he said softly. 'Where's the path? How can we capitalise on this shift? It's in this piece of writing, in my opinion; this simple sincere piece written three decades ago. Just let's.. look.'~~

~~He raised his finger and highlighted another fragment of text.~~

~~*'And there's kind of a loveliness about it which makes you always conscious of your connection with the physical world. Your brain pauses for a second and re-discovers the world for you. This is the first time you've got in a car with these legs, and it feels different. The first time you've walked downstairs. The first time you've chugged up a hill. The first time you've tried to run, hoping that maybe just this once you'd be able to run. But it reminds you for just a few days that*~~

Walking the Walk, 2050 by Fiona Capp

When Christopher got the job with Pro-aesthetic as an imagineer he was over moon and so was I. He had spent two, dispiriting years searching for work after graduating in Imagineering – in my day we called it marketing – and copping knock back after knock back. A few times, he reached the second round of interviews, but that was as far as it went. I had started to worry that he was too good for the world and would never get the break he deserved.

At school, his teachers often described him as 'impressionable' and 'easily lead' which meant that he occasionally got into strife. But he was a sweet natured boy and they could see this. He desperately wanted to be popular, to be with the in-group, which made him somewhat slavish in his attention to fashion and the latest trends. In job interviews, he was always trying to say the right thing and I suspect that he came across as a little too eager to please. At school, the nastier kids used to call him a suck.

If only he were only given the chance to prove himself, I was sure he would shine. But now, when I look back on what happened, I can't help feeling that Pro-aesthetic chose him precisely because they saw him as pliable, an employee who would sacrifice his best interests for the sake of holding on to his job; a perfect mannequin for the company.

When Christopher started at Pro-aesthetic, the company was best known for consolidating its market share in prosthetics for diabetics, which was ravaging the Industrialised world. Back in the 20s, its primary market was amputees who were victims of old 20th century ordinance – the landmines that peppered warzones across the planet. With global viable farmland shrinking so much after the millennium, people were forced to venture back onto those zones – across Africa and Asia mostly – and the company had a stream of candidates who were will, desperate even, for new improved limbs to replace their old ones.

Before applying for the job, Christopher did his homework on the company's biggest innovations – NewSkin, a knee joint that won them an international prize, Carefree Barefoot with indestructible synthetic soles and

SuperReal Prosthetic Pro, the gamechanger which was so lifelike and responsive it could reproduce the marks caused by sock elastic.

During his first few months at Pro-aesthetic, he was on a high and a bit strung-out, as if all the hype he was imbibing and channelling had gone to his head. He would come home from work chattering wildly about the need to 'harness emotional surges and the craving for specialness' and 'improved enhancement options for discerning clients'. The technology had become so sophisticated, he said, there was no limit to what artificial limbs could do. When he started talking about 'pro-active cosmetic enhancement' it meant nothing to me. As far as I was concerned, it was just more meaningless jargon. But Christopher had always loved playing with words and it was his job to dream this stuff up. I didn't want to be a wet blanket, so I told him it sounded fascinating and that as a consumer I might be open to the idea, even though I had no idea what it meant.

I remember him looking at me keenly when I said this. 'You really think so?' he said. 'It was Jared's idea. He's a genius at the big picture.' I knew who Jared was because Christopher was always going on about him, the visionary CEO who was so far ahead of the rest of them.

After Christopher had been working at Pro-aesthetic for a year, he took four weeks holiday. I was hoping we could spend a week together at the little seaside resort where his father and I used to take him for summer holidays when he was a boy. But he said that Jared had something big planned for him and the other Imagineers. A bonding holiday he called it. It was important, he said, that the executive team demonstrate their brand loyalty, that they set the trend. It was all about fashion, art and primal attraction.

I found it hard to see what fashion, art or primal attraction had to do with prosthetic limbs, although I did have an inkling that there could be something fetishistic about them. I supposed he was referring to the interactive tattooing and self-tanning apps incorporated into some of these limbs. I liked to think that I was up on all the company's latest innovations but I clearly, I didn't have a clue. That's painfully obvious to me now.

The day he came home from his holidays, it was over 35 degrees, with a dry northerly scouring the streets. I remember it vividly because Christopher was wearing a long-sleeve shirt and jeans, which was unusual for him. In this kind of weather, he'd normally be in shorts and a t-shirt. As he walked up the hallway towards me, there was something odd about his gait, as if he was terribly stiff. I assumed it was because of all that cross-country running he said they were going to be doing, although I couldn't understand why he looked so pale. Surely he would have got plenty of sunshine?

When I put my arms out to give him a hug, he tensed and stepped backwards, as if he didn't want to be touched.

'I'm a bit sore, Mum,' he said.

'Have you strained anything?'

'A hammy, maybe. Nothing serious.'

Looking across at him it suddenly struck me he looked taller than he had four weeks ago. He was only 24 and I wondered if he'd had a growth spurt. Or perhaps I was shrinking. My mother lost half an inch every decade after 50.

'I promise I'll be gentle,' I said to him as I put my arms around him.

He reluctantly returned the embrace, his head turned to one side, a pained look on his face. I knew as soon as I felt his arms they were different in a way that four weeks holiday couldn't explain. He had always been rather scrawny. For a period in his late teens, he went to the gym twice a week in an attempt to build what he considered a more manly physique. But working out didn't transform him in the way he'd hoped and he soon gave up. 'There's nothing wrong with being lean,' I told him. At school, they called him the Skelly, short for skeleton. He'd never had a girlfriend and was convinced it was because he was so 'scraggy' as he put it, so thin.

Before he could pull away, I grabbed him by the shoulders, shoulders that didn't seem to belong to him. They were so muscular and broad, with biceps that bulged through his shirt.

Shocked, I whispered, 'Have you been taking steroids?'

'If only!' he spat bitterly, and broke down. He sank on to the couch and put his face in his hands. That's when I noticed them, his hands. Hands I had first seen when he was in my womb. Hands I had tickled and held and kissed since the day he was born. I would them recognise anywhere.

And they weren't his.

Walking the Walk, 2050

When Christopher got the job with Pro-aesthetic as an imagineer he was over moon and so was I. He had spent two, dispiriting years searching for work after graduating in Imagineering – in my day we called it marketing – and copping knock back after knock back. A few times, he reached the second round of interviews, but that was as far as it went. I had started to worry that he was too good for the world and would never get the break he deserved.

At school, his teachers often described him as 'impressionable' and 'easily lead' which meant that he occasionally got into strife. But he was a sweet natured boy and they could see this. He desperately wanted to be popular, to be with the in-group, which made him somewhat slavish in his attention to fashion and the latest trends. In job interviews, he was always trying to say the right thing and I suspect that he came across as a little too eager to please. At school, the nastier kids used to call him a suck.

If only he were only given the chance to prove himself, I was sure he would shine. But now, when I look back on what happened, I can't help feeling that Pro-aesthetic chose him precisely because they saw him as pliable, an employee who would sacrifice his best interests for the sake of holding on to his job; a perfect mannequin for the company.

When Christopher started at Pro-aesthetic, the company was best known for consolidating its market share in prosthetics for diabetics, which was ravaging the Industrialised world. Back in the 20s, its primary market was amputees who were victims of old 20th century ordinance—the landmines that peppered warzones across the planet. With global viable farmland shrinking so much after the millennium, people were forced to venture back onto those zones—across Africa and Asia mostly—and the company had a stream of candidates who were will, desperate even, for new improved limbs to replace their old ones.

Before applying for the job, Christopher did his homework on the company's biggest innovations—NewSkin, a knee joint that won them an international prize, Carefree Barefoot with indestructible synthetic soles and SuperReal Prosthetic Pro, the gamechanger which was so lifelike and responsive it could reproduce the marks caused by sock elastic.

During his first few months at Pro-aesthetic, he was on a high and a bit strung-out, as if all the hype he was imbibing and channelling had gone to his head. He would come home from work chattering wildly about the need to 'harness emotional surges and the craving for specialness' and 'improved enhancement options for discerning clients'. The technology had become so sophisticated, he said, there was no limit to what artificial limbs could do. When he started talking about 'pro-active cosmetic enhancement' it meant nothing to me. As far as I was concerned, it was just more meaningless jargon. But Christopher had always loved playing with words and it was his job to dream this stuff up. I didn't want to be a wet blanket, so I told him it sounded fascinating and that as a consumer I might be open to the idea, even though I had no idea what it meant.

I remember him looking at me keenly when I said this. 'You really think so?' he said. 'It was Jared's idea. He's a genius at the big picture.' I knew who Jared was because Christopher was always going on about him, the visionary CEO who was so far ahead of the rest of them.

After Christopher had been working at Pro-aesthetic for a year, he took four weeks holiday. I was hoping we could spend a week together at the little seaside resort where his father and I used to take him for summer holidays when he was a boy. But he said that Jared had something big planned for him and the other Imagineers. A bonding holiday he called it. It was important, he said, that the executive team demonstrate their brand loyalty, that they set the trend. It was all about fashion, art and primal attraction.

I found it hard to see what fashion, art or primal attraction had to do with prosthetic limbs, although I did have an inkling that there could be something fetishistic about them. I supposed he was referring to the interactive tattooing and self-tanning apps incorporated into some of these limbs. I liked to think that I was up on all the company's latest innovations but I clearly, I didn't have a clue. That's painfully obvious to me now.

The day he came home from his holidays, it was over 35 degrees, with a

~~dry northerly scouring the streets. I remember it vividly because Christopher was wearing a long-sleeve shirt and jeans, which was unusual for him. In this kind of weather, he'd normally be in shorts and a t-shirt. As he walked up the hallway towards me, there was something odd about his gait, as if he was terribly stiff. I assumed it was because of all that cross-country running he said they were going to be doing, although I couldn't understand why he looked so pale. Surely he would have got plenty of sunshine?~~

~~When I put my arms out to give him a hug, he tensed and stepped backwards, as if he didn't want to be touched.~~

~~'I'm a bit sore, Mum,' he said.~~

~~'Have you strained anything?'~~

~~'A hammy, maybe. Nothing serious.'~~

~~Looking across at him it suddenly struck me he looked taller than he had four weeks ago. He was only 24 and I wondered if he'd had a growth spurt. Or perhaps I was shrinking. My mother lost half an inch every decade after 50.~~

~~'I promise I'll be gentle,' I said to him as I put my arms around him.~~

~~He reluctantly returned the embrace, his head turned to one side, a pained look on his face. I knew as soon as I felt his arms they were different in a way that four weeks holiday couldn't explain. He had always been rather scrawny. For a period in his late teens, he went to the gym twice a week in an attempt to build what he considered a more manly physique. But working-out didn't transform him in the way he'd hoped and he soon gave up. 'There's nothing wrong with being lean,' I told him. At school, they called him the Skelly, short for skeleton. He'd never had a girlfriend and was convinced it was because he was so 'scraggy' as he put it, so thin.~~

~~Before he could pull away, I grabbed him by the shoulders, shoulders that didn't seem to belong to him. They were so muscular and broad, with biceps that bulged through his shirt.~~

~~Shocked, I whispered, 'Have you been taking steroids?'~~

~~'If only!' he spat bitterly, and broke down. He sank on to the couch and put his face in his hands. That's when I noticed then, his hands. Hands I had first seen when he was in my womb. Hands I had tickled and held and kissed since the day he was born. I would them recognise anywhere.~~

~~And they weren't his.~~

From The Australian Dictionary of Literary Biography

Rand Washington (Bruce Alfred Boggs) (1919-2000)

Rand Washington was one of the most prolific and controversial science fiction writers in the history of the genre. Best known for his once hugely popular *Cor* series of science fiction novels and short stories, and his extreme views on race, gender and politics, Washington was born Bruce Alfred Boggs on 11 August 1919 in Wollongong, NSW, exactly nine months after the armistice which brought an end to the First World War. He was to claim later in life that the last shot fired in anger during the Great War had been his father impregnating his mother just before 11am on Armistice Day.

Washington's father was a police constable, and his mother worked as a maid in one of the wealthier areas of Wollongong. The writer's childhood was defined by, on the one hand, the frequent, brutal beatings he received from his father, and on the other, his endless reading and rereading of the novels of H.G. Wells which his mother first borrowed, then stole, from the houses she worked in. Washington's critics have been quick to seize on these facts to explain the sadomasochistic bent of much of his fiction, especially the *Cor* sequence.

The petty thefts of Washington's mother were eventually discovered by a gardener working for the same household, leading to her dismissal from service and her turning to alcohol. This would lead to her death in 1930 from cirrhosis at the age of only thirty-nine, when Washington was eleven years old. Washington was never to forget the gardener, or the fact he was aboriginal.

By the time of his mother's death, Washington, having all but memorised the works of H.G. Wells, began to search out the few pulp magazines that reached Australia from America, months and sometimes years after publication. His discovery of the pulps was to have an enormous effect on Washington, both physically and psychologically. Seven months after completing a coupon cut out from *Spicy Detective Stories* and sending it to New York, Washington

From The Australian Dictionary of Literary Biography

~~Rand Washington (Bruce Alfred Boggs) (1919-2000) by Ryan O'Neill~~

Rand Washington was one of the most prolific and controversial science fiction writers in the history of the genre. Best known for his once hugely popular *Cor* series of science fiction novels and short stories, and his extreme views on race, gender and politics, Washington was born Bruce Alfred Boggs on 11 August 1919 in Wollongong, NSW, exactly nine months after the armistice which brought an end to the First World War. He was to claim later in life that the last shot fired in anger during the Great War had been his father impregnating his mother just before 11am on Armistice Day.

Washington's father was a police constable, and his mother worked as a maid in one of the wealthier areas of Wollongong. The writer's childhood was defined by, on the one hand, the frequent, brutal beatings he received from his father, and on the other, his endless reading and rereading of the novels of H. G. Wells which his mother first borrowed, then stole, from the houses she worked in. Washington's critics have been quick to seize on these facts to explain the sadomasochistic bent of much of his fiction, especially the *Cor* sequence.

The petty thefts of Washington's mother were eventually discovered by a gardener working for the same household, leading to her dismissal from service and her turning to alcohol. This would lead to her death in 1930 from cirrhosis at the age of only thirty-nine, when Washington was eleven years old. Washington was never to forget the gardener, or the fact he was aboriginal. By the time of his mother's death, Washington, having all but memorised the works of H. G. Wells, began to search out the few pulp magazines that reached Australia from America, months and sometimes years after publication. His discovery of the pulps was to have an enormous effect on Washington, both physically and psychologically. Seven months after completing a coupon cut out from *Spicy Detective Stories* and sending it to New York, Washington received the first instalment of 'Hercules Strong's Twelve Lessons to Physical Perfection.' After diligently following Strong's instructions for three years, Washington had, by the time he was fifteen, succeeded in transforming his physique to such an extent that (he once claimed) he was offered a job as strongman when a circus visited the town.

Washington's reading ranged across every genre the pulps offered, from cowboy stories, wilderness romance, and medical dramas, to science fiction, fantasy and horror. He was an early correspondent of H. P. Lovecraft, whose work he first came across in the October, 1933 issue of *Weird Tales*. Washington's first short stories were in the horror genre, and Lovecraft, always generous with his time, offered to critique them. Though these early stories have not survived, Lovecraft's responses have, and demonstrate the Providence writer's acute literary judgement tempered with an endless patience at Washington's absolute ignorance of grammar and punctuation. As well as advising Washington to buy a dictionary and thesaurus, Lovecraft also warned Washington that filling his stories with extremist views on race could, as he knew from personal experience, alienate editors. Washington did not listen. Eventually, even Lovecraft became wearied by the young Australian writer's endless jeremiads against 'the mongrel races' and the correspondence petered out after two years. Washington always maintained that this was because he had outgrown Lovecraft and his genre, and had discovered his true love, science fiction.

Surprisingly, Washington's last letter to Lovecraft makes no mention of Washington's father's death, which occurred two days before the missive was dated. Washington's father was killed on 6 January 1935, his neck broken and his head almost torn off while on night patrol in the warehouse district. The murder was never solved. With the insurance payout from the Police Union, Washington moved to Sydney, rented a one-room flat in Kings Cross and devoted all his time to writing. Washington was nothing if not prolific. In the second half of 1935 he wrote an estimated 500,000 words, submitting ten novellas and forty short stories to Australian pulps ranging from *Thrilling Housekeeping Yarns* to *Spooky Bush Tales*. All these submissions, under the name Bruce Boggs, were swiftly rejected. The absolute dismissal of all his work only led him to redouble his efforts, as he wrote an average of one million words a year from 1936 to the outbreak of the war.

In July 1936, one month after adopting the pen-name, 'Rand Washington' the young writer finally made his first sale, 'The Rockets of Uranus V' to *Bonzer Science Stories* for £5.

This sale encouraged him to focus entirely on the burgeoning, and increasingly lucrative, Australian pulp science fiction market. *Bonzer Science Stories* was one of two dozen pulps published by the Siegfried Press, founded, managed and edited by James Smith (born Johannes Schmidt, Munich, 1882) a German war veteran who had immigrated to Australia in 1921. Smith was keen to expand into the novel market, and after accepting and publishing nine stories by Washington in 1936, he arranged to meet with the young writer in January, 1937 to discuss ideas for longer works. It was at this meeting that Washington was first introduced to the tenets of National Socialism. Smith presented the young writer with a signed copy of Hitler's *Mein Kampf*, to which the Siegfried Press held Australian publishing rights. The result of Hitler's, and to a lesser extent, Smith's influence on Washington's hitherto virulent but directionless racism can be seen in Washington's first novel, *Whiteman of Cor*, published in July 1937.

This story, the first in the seemingly endless *Cor* cycle, was to set the template for those that followed. 'Buck Whiteman' a space scout employed by the nation of 'Ausmerica' to seek new worlds for colonisation, is lost and shipwrecked on the hostile desert planet (read, 'Australian Bush) of Cor. Here, the 'white race' led by the love interest in all the *Cor* novels, Princess BelleFemme Blanch, have been overthrown and enslaved by the 'Agarboilin,' described as 'a savage, untrustworthy, genetically inferior race of evil blacks.' After rescuing the princess and inciting a rebellion, Whiteman leads the new 'White Masters of Cor' on a mission of extermination against their erstwhile 'dusky overlords.' Despite the blatant, sickening racism directed towards Australia's indigenous inhabitants which permeates every word of the *Cor* 'saga,' and a writing style that has been most generously described as 'sub-literate', *Whiteman of Cor* was an immediate popular success, being reprinted six times in 1937 alone.

Smith immediately ordered Washington back to the typewriter, and over the next two years, a further twenty five *Cor* novels appeared, first serialised in *Bonzer Science Stories* and its newly launched sister publications, *Bonzer Scientifiction Tales* and *Astounding True Blue Science* before being published as standalone novels. All were bestsellers, and, along with the rapid translation and publication of the *Cor* books into German in 1938, beginning with *Der Weise Mann Von Cor*, helped make Smith a millionaire. Unfortunately for Washington, he had signed the rights to all present and future *Cor* novels over to Smith in June 1937 for £200.

Sadly, Smith's good fortune was not to last. The outbreak of war in 1939, the paper shortages that followed, and most damningly, Smith's continuing and vocal support of Hitler, led to the virtual bankruptcy of Smith's publishing empire by 1941. One year later, though his company had just posted a small profit, Smith committed suicide by leaping through the closed window of his tenth floor Sydney Harbour apartment. Fortunately for Washington, Smith had written a new will on the night he died, naming Washington as his sole beneficiary, and most importantly for the writer, returning the *Cor* rights to their creator. In another stroke of good luck, Washington was exempted from military service because of his work in publishing, a reserved occupation.

Throughout the war years Washington rebuilt the Siegfried Press (renamed in 1943 as the Fountainhead Press) primarily by capitalising on the public's fear of Japan. *Whiteman of Yellos*, the beginning of a new series, saw Buck Whiteman and his insipid princess journey to the neighbouring planet of Yellos, where 'yellow demons' had overthrown the race of 'Purewhites.' At the same time, a new line of pulps, including *A Bonzer Selection* and *Bonzer Down on the Farm Stories* took advantage of the public's nostalgia for simpler times. By the end of the Second World War, Washington was solely responsible for writing a dozen science-fiction pulps, editing a further twenty bush, romance and medical themed pulps, and overseeing the ghostwriting of the latest Yellos novels. Exhausted, he decided to hire an editor to look after the company's increasingly profitable romance line which included *Sheilas in Love*, *Nurse Sheila Romances* and *Spicy Sheila True Confessions.* In June 1946, Washington arranged to meet with J. R. Hardacre, the most prolific contributor of stories to the romance pulps, to offer him the position. Washington was stunned to discover that Hardacre was actually a woman, real name Joyce Reith (born London, 1920. See entry for Washington, Joyce).

Though aware Washington's novels, stories and editorials were full of references to the weakness and helplessness of the female sex, Reith still accepted the offered role.

Washington proposed to Reith several times throughout 1947 and 1948, but it was only after Reith's father was forced to declare bankruptcy after losing his uninsured bookshop in Newtown to a mysterious fire that she finally accepted. Washington and Reith married in June, 1948, the same month that the sales of Reith's romance pulps exceeded, for the first time, those of Washington's science fiction magazines. After their marriage Washington made his father-in-law a substantial loan, an act of generosity Washington memorialised in several editorials in Fountainhead pulps.

The birth of the couple's son, Peter, in November 1950, inspired Washington to establish a new line of pulps to cater for the post-war baby boom, led by *Stupendous Bubba Stories*. The romance and baby bubble, expertly edited and marketed by Joyce Washington, was to continue until the mid-1950s, and was, by that time, all that was keeping the Fountainhead Press solvent. In 1956 it had become obvious to Washington that the Australian pulp market was dying, and he reluctantly sold his company to a competitor for £5,000.

Though several more *Cor* and *Yellos* novels appeared in the final years of the 1950s, Washington was to complain in letters to the few Australian SF pulps still active that it was becoming increasingly difficult to get his work published. He blamed a 'shadowy Aboriginal cabal in the publishing world' for the denouncing of *Slave Girls of Cor* as 'a literary embarrassment, and a revolting stain on the national character' in a book review in *The Sydney Morning Herald*, on 12 June 1959. Though conservative commentators such as Graham Nutt leapt to Washington's defence, arguing that the *Cor* novels were 'a unique attempt to create a mythology for this great country, which has never had one,' Washington never completed another *Cor* novel after 1960. Instead he turned his attentions to non-fiction, writing a number of bestselling travel books including, *I Got the Wog in Greece* and *Who Needs Italy?* the popularity of which only increased after it was revealed Washington had never set foot in the countries he wrote so scathingly about. Although non-fiction proved a steady source of income, Washington decided to return to science fiction in 1966, in response to reading Michael Moorcock's seminal work of the New Wave,

Elric of Melniboné. On seeing the cover of Moorcock's novel in the bookshop, with its gaunt albino protagonist, Washington bought it believing it to be a tribute to his *Cor* series. Instead he was appalled to discover the adventures of Moorcock's melancholy, sexually ambiguous, drug-taking anti-hero, leading to Washington's vow, in a 1968 letter, 'to reclaim SF!'

Washington's efforts were not successful. In 1969 his new novel, *Hip Spaceways to Happeningtown* was rejected by every mainstream SF publisher in Australia and America. Disheartened, Washington destroyed the novel, an act SF critic Damien Johnson characterised as, 'Rand Washington's one lasting contribution to Science Fiction.' Washington spent 1968 researching for his next project, which he decided was to be an exposé of organised religion. *Profits in Prophets: How to Make a Million from Founding Your Own Religion* was published in July 1969, to low sales and lukewarm reviews.

Six months later, while camping near Uluru, Washington claimed to have experienced a vision of a 'Universal Galactic Controller' who existed outside of our spacetime continuum, and who had chosen

Washington to spread his 'Gospell' (sic). This Gospell was found by Washington, neatly typed, under a rock near his campsite. Many ridiculed Washington's conversion, paralleling exactly as it did the instructions he had given in his book on religion published earlier that year. Yet Washington's new religion, 'Transvoidism' proved surprisingly popular among the Sydney elite. At the height of the Transvoidist craze in October 1970, at least a hundred individuals, including the son of a media baron, and the wife of a state senator, assembled at Washington's recently purchased compound near Gloucester, NSW, to hear him preach. The precise doctrines of Transvoidism were shrouded in mystery, though it was rumoured that by following its tenets as given in the Gospell, eternal life through would be gifted to the faithful who had attained the 'fifth level.' However, only the most generous of adherents were initiated past the second level. Washington's wife, Joyce, reached the fourth level. Only Washington was understood to have reached the fifth.

Washington's commitment to Transvoidism was tested by the return of his son, Peter, from fighting with the Australian Defence Force in Vietnam in July 1971. Peter had been maimed after stepping on a land mine in Hoi An, and had lost his both legs and his left arm. In a sermon he had delivered shortly before news of his son's injuries had reached Australia, Washington claimed that the Universal Controller had recently gifted him with several special powers, including the ability to cure cancer, and to regrow damaged organs and tissue. After Peter's arrival at the compound from hospital in 1972, Washington's followers became increasingly insistent he exhibit his powers by regrowing his son's legs. Washington put off the demonstration several times throughout 1973, claiming the Universal Controller would not approve of the resulting publicity. Finally, on 6 February 1974 Washington announced he would perform the regeneration ceremony the next day. That night all eighteen of Washington's remaining disciples were struck down with severe stomach pains and diarrhoea. At first insisting that this was a sign of the Universal Controller's displeasure, Washington finally admitted doctoring the evening meal with laxatives. He was arrested on 7 May 1975, and charged with reckless endangerment. Washington famously claimed he told the police, 'They were giving me the shits, so I gave them the shits.' However, transcripts of Washington's police interviews do not include this statement; only his pleas to be released, and his attempts to blame his wife, are recorded.

Washington was sentenced to three months in prison and after his release in February, 1975 he returned to Gloucester, and his wife and son. Legal action brought about by his former adherents had almost bankrupted the family, and Washington was therefore keen to make some money by writing. He toyed with writing another *Cor* novel, provisionally titled, *Bad Trip on Cor*, but soon abandoned the idea. In fact, despite his announcing the beginning or completion of several novels throughout the rest of the 1970s, Washington published nothing, instead living off his son's disability and army pensions.

It was not until 1982 that the short story 'Walking the Walk 2050', generally considered to be Washington's best work, appeared in the February issue of the short-lived but influential Australian SF journal, *Up Above, Down Under*. The story, set as the title suggests in the year 2050, is narrated by a unnamed mother, who watches with pride, and then growing alarm, as her son, Christopher, finds work as an 'imagineer' at 'Pro-aesthetic,' a multinational company specialising in creating replacement limbs for amputees, as well as synthetic skin, bones and joints. As the story progresses, it becomes clear that Pro-aesthetic intend to market their replacement limbs as fashion accessories for the young and impressionable. The story ends with Christopher's mother discovering that her son has had his limbs replaced by Pro-aesthetic artificial arms and legs. In the celebrated climax, the weeping mother can derive no comfort from her son stroking her hair with a hand that does not belong to him.

'Walking the Walk 2050' was a radical departure for Washington in almost every way. Throughout his dozens of novels and hundreds of short stories, he had never employed a female narrator before; in fact his female characters were nothing more to him than 'walking wombs,' as he confided in a 1959 letter. Yet the character of the mother in the story is evoked with astonishing sensitivity, and her final, horrified realisation at what has happened to her son is deeply moving. Critics have suggested that the newfound subtlety and sensitivity displayed in this story was

Washington's reaction to the horrific injuries his son suffered in Vietnam. This theory is, nonetheless, undercut by Washington's private letters written around the time that 'Walking the Walk 2050' was written, in which he describes his son as a 'mewling, mollycoddled, mother's boy, who should have lost his head along with his legs.' 'Walking the Walk 2050' is also notable for its writing style, which included more complex sentences, similes, and metaphors than all of Washington's millions of earlier published words combined. The story also marks the only time Washington chose to invent ideas rather than steal them; his neologisms 'imagineer' and 'newskin' were immediately embraced by science fiction writers in Australia and beyond. To date at least a hundred stories have been set in the 'Walking the Walk 2050' universe, including China Mieville's metafictional 'Talking the Talk 2050' and M. John Harrison's savage parody, 'Walking until 20:50.'

Puzzlingly, shortly after publication of 'Walking the Walk 2050', Washington wrote a furious letter to the editor of *Up Above, Down Under*, disowning the story as a 'mere woman's daydream,' and 'turgid piece of touchy-feely non-SF.' It was only when 'Walking the Walk

2050' was selected for inclusion in *The Best Australian Science Fiction 1982*, and subsequently shortlisted for the Hugo Award, that he withdrew his protest and accepted the story as his own. On the strength of 'Walking the Walk 2050' winning the Hugo for Best Short Story in 1983, Washington was offered a contract by Tor to write three Ace Star Specials. The first two of these novels, *A Kaleidoscope of Rockets* (1984) a postmodern deconstruction of Golden Age SF, and the feminist fantasy novel, *The Sorceress of the Dawn* (1986) with their inventive plots, complex characters and intelligent exploration of race and gender received excellent, if bewildered reviews from critics who had long dismissed Washington as a racist hack. Though the third contracted novel, the autobiographical *The Woman Behind the Android* was announced, it was never completed. After Joyce Washington died in 1987, from severe head trauma after slipping in the shower, a grief-stricken Washington announced his immediate retirement from fiction writing.

Over the next several years Washington was known to be working on his autobiography, *The Last Shot*, co-written with his son, Peter. His opinion pieces, usually in praise of the government's immigration policy, appeared sporadically in national broadsheets, until his death. Washington lived to see his *Cor* series enjoying a new surge of popularity amid disaffected youth in France, Germany and the southern United States. *The Last Shot* was left unfinished as Washington suffered a stroke on 14 May 1995, which left him paralysed, mute, and completely dependent on his son for the last years of Washington's life. Peter had been given full control over Washington's literary estate just before the writer was struck down by illness.

In early 1996, Peter Washington founded the 'Rand Washington Trust,' a charitable organisation which uses the not inconsiderable royalties from the *Cor* series to fund various progressive causes, from campaigning for gay marriage, to Aboriginal Land Rights and legal representation for asylum seekers. Until his death at the turn of the century, Washington, frail and in a wheelchair, became a fixture in demonstrations for social justice throughout Australia, always accompanied by his son.

Rand Washington died on 24 February 2000 at the Sydney Gay and Lesbian Mardi Gras. In accordance with his will, he was buried in Gloucester beside his wife, Joyce, with a copy of *Whiteman of Cor* in his coffin.

~~From The Australian Dictionary of Literary~~ Biography of a White Man
Rand Washington ~~(Bruce Alfred Boggs) (1919-2000)~~

~~Rand Washington was one of the most prolific and controversial science fiction writers in the history of the genre. Best known for his once hugely popular *Cor* series of science fiction novels and short stories, and his extreme views on race, gender and politics, Washington was born Bruce Alfred Boggs on 11 August 1919 in Wollongong, NSW, exactly nine months after the armistice which brought an end to the First World War. He was to claim later in life~~ said that the
last shot fired in anger
during the Great War
had been his father impregnating his mother
just before 11am on Armistice Day.

~~Washington's father was a police constable, and his mother worked as a maid in one of the wealthier areas of Wollongong. The writer's childhood was defined by, on the one hand, the~~ His life ricocheted between
frequent, brutal beatings ~~he received from his father, and on the other, his~~ and endless reading and rereading
of the novels of H.G. Wells ~~which his mother first borrowed, then stole, from the houses she worked in. Washington's critics have been quick to seize on these facts to explain the sadomasochistic bent of much of his fiction, especially the *Cor* sequence.~~

~~The petty thefts of Washington's mother were eventually discovered by a gardener working for the same household, leading to her dismissal from service and her turning to alcohol. This would lead to her death in 1930 from cirrhosis at the age of only thirty-nine, when Washington was eleven years old. Washington was never to forget the gardener, or the fact he was aboriginal. By the time of his mother's death, Washington, having all but memorised the works of H.G. Wells, began to search out the few pulp magazines that reached Australia from America, months and sometimes years after publication. His discovery of the pulps was to have an enormous effect on Washington, both physically and psychologically. Seven months after completing a coupon cut out from *Spicy Detective Stories* and sending it to New York, Washington received the first instalment of 'Hercules Strong's Twelve Lessons to Physical Perfection.' After diligently following Strong's instructions for three years, Washington had, by the time he was fifteen, succeeded in transforming his physique to such an extent that (he once claimed) he was offered a job as strongman when a circus visited the town.~~

~~Washington's reading ranged across every genre the pulps offered, from cowboy stories, wilderness romance, and medical dramas, to science fiction, fantasy and horror. He was an early correspondent of H.P. Lovecraft, whose work he first came across in the October, 1933 issue of *Weird Tales*. Washington's first short stories were in the horror genre, and Lovecraft, always generous with his time, offered to critique them. Though these early stories have not survived, Lovecraft's responses have, and demonstrate the Providence writer's acute literary judgement tempered with an endless patience at Washington's absolute ignorance of grammar and punctuation. As well as advising Washington to buy a dictionary and thesaurus, Lovecraft also warned~~

~~Washington's commitment to Transvoidism was tested by the return of his son, Peter, from fighting with the Australian Defence Force in Vietnam in July 1971. Peter had been maimed after stepping on a land mine in Hoi An, and had lost his both legs and his left arm. In a sermon he had delivered shortly before news of his son's injuries had reached Australia, Washington claimed that the Universal Controller had recently gifted him with several special powers, including the ability to cure cancer, and to regrow damaged organs and tissue. After Peter' arrival at the compound from hospital in 1972, Washington's followers became increasingly insistent he exhibit his powers by regrowing his son's legs. Washington put off the demonstration several times throughout 1973, claiming the Universal Controller would not approve of the resulting publicity. Finally, on 6 February 1974 Washington announced he would perform the regeneration ceremony the next day. That night all eighteen of Washington's remaining disciples were struck down with severe stomach pains and diarrhoea. At first insisting that this was a sign of the Universal Controller's displeasure, Washington finally admitted~~

doctoring the evening meal with laxatives. He was arrested on 7 May 1975, and charged with reckless endangerment. Washington famously claimed he told the police, 'They were giving me the shits, so I gave them the shits.' However, transcripts of Washington's police interviews do not include this statement; only his pleas to be released, and his attempts to blame his wife, are recorded.

Washington was sentenced to three months in prison and after his release in February, 1975 he returned to Gloucester, and his wife and son. Legal action brought about by his former adherents had almost bankrupted the family, and Washington was therefore keen to make some money by writing. He toyed with writing another *Cor* novel, provisionally titled, *Bad Trip on Cor*, but soon abandoned the idea. In fact, despite his announcing the beginning or completion of several novels throughout the rest of the 1970s, Washington published nothing, instead living off his son's disability and army pensions.

It was not until 1982 that the short story 'Walking the Walk 2050', generally considered to be Washington's best work, appeared in the February issue of the short-lived but influential Australian SF journal, *Up Above, Down Under*. The story, set as the title suggests in the year 2050, is narrated by a unnamed mother, who watches with pride, and then growing alarm, as her son, Christopher, finds work as an 'imagineer' at 'Pro-aesthetic,' a multinational company specialising in creating replacement limbs for amputees, as well as synthetic skin, bones and joints. As the story progresses, it becomes clear that Pro-aesthetic intend to market their replacement limbs as fashion accessories for the young and impressionable. The story ends with Christopher's mother discovering that her son has had his limbs replaced by Pro-aesthetic artificial arms and legs. In the celebrated climax, the weeping mother can derive no comfort from her son stroking her hair with a hand that does not belong to him.

'Walking the Walk 2050' was a radical departure for Washington in almost every way. Throughout his dozens of novels and hundreds of short stories, he had never employed a female narrator before; in fact his female characters were nothing more to him than 'walking wombs,' as he confided in a 1959 letter. Yet the character of the mother in the story is evoked with astonishing sensitivity, and her final, horrified realisation at what has happened to her son is deeply moving. Critics have suggested that the newfound subtlety and sensitivity displayed in this story was Washington's reaction to the horrific injuries his son suffered in Vietnam. This theory is, nonetheless, undercut by Washington's private letters written around the time that 'Walking the Walk 2050' was written, in which he describes his son as a 'mewling, mollycoddled, mother's boy, who should have lost his head along with his legs.' 'Walking the Walk 2050' is also notable for its writing style, which included more complex sentences, similes, and metaphors than all of Washington's millions of earlier published words combined. The story also marks the only time Washington chose to invent ideas rather than steal them; his neologisms 'imagineer' and 'newskin' were immediately embraced by science fiction writers in Australia and beyond. To date at least a hundred stories have been set in the 'Walking the Walk 2050' universe, including China Mieville's metafictional 'Talking the Talk 2050' and M. John Harrison's savage parody, 'Walking until 20:50.' announced, it was never completed.

After Joyce Washington died in 1987, from severe head trauma after slipping in the shower, a grief-stricken Washington announced his immediate retirement from fiction writing.

Over the next several years Washington was known to be working on his autobiography, *The Last Shot*, co-written with his son, Peter. His opinion pieces, usually in praise of the Liberal Party's immigration policy, appeared sporadically in *The Australian*, until his death. Washington lived to see his *Cor* series enjoying a new surge of popularity amid disaffected youth in France, Germany and the southern United States. *The Last Shot* was left unfinished as Washington suffered a stroke on 14 May 1995, which left him paralysed, mute, and completely dependent on his son for the last years of Washington's life. Peter had been given full control over Washington's literary estate just before the writer was struck down by illness.

Biography of a White Man by Krissy Kneen

Rand Washington
said that the last shot fired in anger
during the Great War
had been his father impregnating his mother
just before 11am on Armistice Day.
His life ricocheted between
frequent, brutal beatings
and endless reading and rereading
of the novels of H. G. Wells

Pulp magazines
trudged for lonely months after their print date,
found Australian shores.
Found Washington.
The young boy cut a coupon
from *Spicy Detective Stories*.
Seven months and all that ocean later
he had *Weird Tales* in his hand.
Weirder tales in his head
and on the page.

Washington stormed into the space-bound battle
with 'the mongrel races'

‘the yellow-skinned terrors’
the dog-men ‘black as tar’.

1935 and six months work
Saw handsome blonde-haired heroes
hacking their way through 500,000 words
of evil dark-skinned alien hoards.

Ten novellas and forty stories
rejected by
Super Weird, *Sounds Spooky*, *Antipodean Worlds*

All the anger fuelled the fire
Inciting passion,
And the writing of *Whiteman of Cor.*

Buck Whiteman and his pale princess
Face the ‘yellow demons’ who have overthrown the race of
‘Purewhites.’
A black stain on the literary history of our great land
or as one devoted reader put it
‘a unique attempt to create a mythology for our great country,
which has, until this day never had a mythology at all’

Six months later, camping near Ayers Rock,
Washington experienced a vision
He stumbled upon the Universal Galactic Controller
and Washington was dragged towards the Truth.

The Truth
neatly typed,
under a rock
near his campsite.

Washington, round-shouldered,
stood at speakers corner
proselytizing to a faithless hoard.
A rocket straight to god
A warp in time
A wormhole the faithful white.
'You will face the yellow demons'
His hands renting the air like claws.
His eyes wild and wide.
His hair nearly all gone now.
His teeth in crumbling pieces.

Taking breath,
(hellfire)
peering, open-mouthed
To the young boy in the audience.

A lad, as pure and pale as he once was.
A shot from a pure blood father into a humble mother
to end all wars,
A cherubim
Shaking his pale locks

At such outrageous prophecies
All the while clutching
An old and battered copy of
The Adventures of Whiteman of Cor

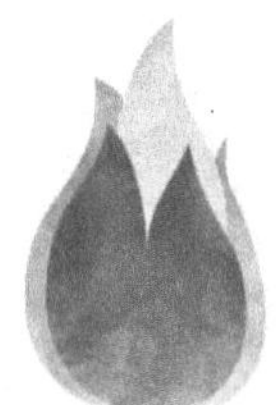

Open Changes

You didn't think we'd leave it there, did you?

Parallel to the web publication of *Lost in Track Changes*, if:book launched a second remix project open to anyone to contribute to and based around flash fiction or 'short short story' form.

Open Changes ran over eight weeks from July to September 2014, beginning with a single piece by Emily Craven. We put the invitation out to the web: remix, rewrite, reimagine, whether in fiction, non-fiction, prose or poetry. As long as the word count didn't exceed the original story, it was eligible.

More than twenty writers contributed to the project as Emily's story twisted, sprawled and mutated through to eleven distinct endpoints.

Published here is Emily's original piece followed by a beautiful poem by Omar Sakr from week eight of the project. To read the many pathways between and beyond, point your web browser to *open.futureofthebook.org.au*.

The Outback Call Girl by Emily Craven

They called her the Outback Call girl, trundling from town to town. Where the beef don't matter and the men think any female face is a beauty. Her only home is the back of a dusty red ute, done up simple, a wide canvas over a deep tray with cotton sheets on a mattress that has seen better days. She wouldn't have it any other way. Why stay in the city where the men are rough brutes who don't know a gentleman from a toilet brush? Where they haggle over price, but give the Barbie's exactly what they ask for, even a tenner more.

In the outback the women are few and far between and a little love is never scorned, the effort of travel never underappreciated, the simple lauded as the height of pleasure. Never to want for food or fuel, her ruddy cheeks sun kissed and the horizon an attainable destination.

A Shutter Mechanism in Reverse by Omar J. Sakr

Jack held the storm aloft
between his thumb and forefinger,
like a single cicada wing.
It rolled slowly, flashed
soundlessly, illuminating
his flesh in an X-ray blink.
His bones forked like lightning strikes
building stairs from waterline
to skyline. His hollow veins
were a broken cellophane window
letting light in edge to edge,
transforming him into
a frozen composite of his father.
He was a tired extension
of the same building,
a fragile membrane,
a whisper in the wind
before the thunderhead
approaching from the south.

Contributors

Fiona Capp

Fiona Capp is the internationally published author of seven books: three works of non-fiction including *That Oceanic Feeling*, which won the 2004 Kibble Award and *My Blood's Country*, a journey through the landscape that inspired the poetry of Judith Wright, and four novels – *Night Surfing*, *Last of the Sane Days*, *Musk & Byrne* and *Gotland.*

Robert Hoge

Robert Hoge has worked as a journalist, a speechwriter, a science communicator for the CSIRO and a political advisor to the former Queensland Premier and Deputy Premier. He has had numerous short stories, articles, interviews and other works published in Australia and overseas. His memoir, *Ugly*, is about growing up ugly and disabled. It's also about bad haircuts and reading and awful teen love poems and underarm bowling as a metaphor for… well, you'll just have to read the book.

Cate Kennedy

Cate Kennedy writes short stories, poetry, non-fiction and is currently working on her second novel. Her work has been published internationally and she is the recipient of the 2010 NSW Premier's Literary Prize People's Choice award for her novel *The World Beneath*, the 2012 Queensland Literary Award for her short story collection *Like a House on Fire* and the 2011 Victorian Premier's Award for her poetry collection *The Taste of River Water*. Her non-fiction work includes *Sing and Don't Cry; a Mexican journal* about her time living and working in a credit cooperative in Mexico. She edited the 2010 and 2011 *Best Australian Stories* anthologies and more recently *New Australian Love Stories.*

Krissy Kneen

Krissy Kneen is the author of the memoir *Affection*, the erotic fiction *Triptych* and the novel *Steeplechase*. Her latest erotic novel is *The Adventures of Holly White and the Incredible Sex Machine*. Her collection of poetry *Eating my Grandmother* won the 2014 Thomas Shapcott Award and will be released in 2015.

Ryan O'Neill

Ryan O'Neill's fiction has appeared in *The Best Australian Stories*, *The Sleepers Almanac*, *Meanjin*, *New Australian Stories*, *Wet Ink*, *Etchings* and *Westerly*. His work has won the Hal Porter and Roland Robinson awards. His book, *The Weight of a Human Heart* has been shortlisted for the 2012 Queensland Literary Prize – Steele Rudd Award. He teaches at the University of Newcastle.

Emily Craven

Emily is a YA author, with her latest novel, *The Grand Adventures of Madeline Cain*, written as though you're reading Facebook. She has appeared in essay collections with Benjamin Law and Carmel Bird, completed a twelve-month mentorship with Isobelle Carmody, and her flash fiction story, 'Always', will be published by *Daily Science Fiction* this year.

Omar J. Sakr

Omar J. Sakr is an Australian poet and writer whose poetry has featured in *Meanjin*, *Cordite Poetry Review*, and *Carve Magazine*, among others. His fiction has also been shortlisted for the Story Wine Prize, and selected for the annual Twitter Fiction Festival.

Simon Groth (Editor)

Simon Groth is a writer and editor of fiction and non. His books include *Concentrate* and *Off The Record: 25 Years of Music Street Press.* His first two novels were shortlisted in the Queensland Premier's Literary Awards and his short fiction has been published in Australia and the United States. As manager of if:book Australia, Simon writes and speaks regularly on the future of the book. He took the role of lead writer for *the 24-Hour Book* and editor for two collections of essays: *Hand Made High Tech* and *The N00bz: New Adventures in Literature.*

www.ingramcontent.com/pod-product-compliance
Lightning Source LLC
Chambersburg PA
CBHW021424110726
47901CB00008B/2292

* 9 7 8 0 6 4 8 3 7 4 6 1 9 *